THE POLITICS
OF KNOWLEDGE

LSE

THE LONDON SCHOOL
OF ECONOMICS AND
POLITICAL SCIENCE ■

The **London School of Economics and Political Science (LSE)** is a world class centre for its concentration of teaching and research across the full range of the social, political and economic sciences. Founded in 1895 by Beatrice and Sidney Webb, LSE has an outstanding reputation for academic excellence.

ISEAS

The **Institute of Southeast Asian Studies (ISEAS)** was established as an autonomous organization in 1968. It is a regional centre dedicated to the study of socio-political, security and economic trends and developments in Southeast Asia and its wider geostrategic and economic environment. The Institute's research programmes are the Regional Economic Studies (RES, including ASEAN and APEC), Regional Strategic and Political Studies (RSPS), and Regional Social and Cultural Studies (RSCS).

ISEAS Publishing, an established academic press, has issued almost 2,000 books and journals. It is the largest scholarly publisher of research about Southeast Asia from within the region. ISEAS Publishing works with many other academic and trade publishers and distributors to disseminate important research and analyses from and about Southeast Asia to the rest of the world.

THE POLITICS
OF KNOWLEDGE

EDITED BY

SAW SWEE-HOCK
DANNY QUAH

LSE THE LONDON SCHOOL
OF ECONOMICS AND
POLITICAL SCIENCE ■

ISEAS

INSTITUTE OF SOUTHEAST ASIAN STUDIES
Singapore

First published in Singapore in 2009 by ISEAS Publishing
Institute of Southeast Asian Studies
30 Heng Mui Keng Terrace
Pasir Panjang
Singapore 119614

E-mail: publish@iseas.edu.sg
Website: <http://bookshop.iseas.edu.sg>

Jointly with London School of Economics and Political Science
Houghton Street, London
WC2A 2AE
UK
Tel: +44 (0)20 7405 7686

The responsibility for facts and opinions in this publication rests exclusively with the authors and their interpretations do not necessarily reflect the views or the policy of the publishers or its supporters.

ISEAS Library Cataloguing-in-Publication Data

The politics of knowledge / edited by Saw Swee-Hock and Danny Quah.
  Papers of the LSE Asia Forum 2008 on "The politics of knowledge" held in Singapore on 11 April 2008.
  1. Knowledge, Sociology of—Political aspects—Congresses.
  I. Saw Swee-Hock, 1931–
  II. Quah, Danny.
  III. LSE Asia Forum (2008 : Singapore)
HM651 P76   2009

ISBN 978-981-230-925-9 (hard cover)
ISBN 978-981-230-933-4 (PDF)

Typeset by Superskill Graphics Pte Ltd
Printed in Singapore by Utopia Press Pte Ltd

CONTENTS

List of Tables		vii
List of Figures		ix
The Contributors		xi
Preface		xv
Foreword		xvii
Messages		xix

Chapter 1   Role of Knowledge in the
Transformation of Asia   1
Lee Hsien Loong

Chapter 2   Understanding the Politics of
Knowledge: The Asian Perspective   12
Saw Swee-Hock and Mustafa Izzuddin

Chapter 3   Truth, Free Speech and Knowledge:
The Human Rights Contribution   34
Conor Gearty

Chapter 4   Knowledge: The Driver of Economic
Growth   57
Danny Quah

Chapter 5   Commerce vs the Common Conflicts
                 over the Commercialisation of
                 Biomedical Knowledge   79
                 Nikolas Rose

Chapter 6   A Global Deal on Climate Change   111
                 Nicholas Stern

Chapter 7   The Changing Politics of Religious
                 Knowledge in Asia: The Case of
                 Indonesia   156
                 John T. Sidel

Index   193

LIST OF TABLES

TABLE 4.1   Fraction of World Gross National Income
            and Absolute Growth, 2005–06
            (at market exchange rates)   63
TABLE 4.2   Poverty, 1981–2004   65

TABLE 6.1   Likelihood (in %) of Exceeding a
            Temperature Increase at Equilibrium   120
TABLE 6.2   Key Elements of A Global Deal:
            Targets and Trade   142
TABLE 6.3   Key Elements of A Global Deal: Funding   143

LIST OF FIGURES

FIGURE 4.1   Market Exchange Rates, 1975–2005   59
FIGURE 4.2   Emerging Asia Held Things Together   60
FIGURE 4.3   World Shares at Market Exchange Rates   61
FIGURE 4.4   Contributors to World Growth, 1975–2006   62
FIGURE 4.5   LSE Student Composition, 2004–07   63
FIGURE 4.6   LSE Foreign Student Composition,
              2004–07   64
FIGURE 4.7   Growth and $1 – Day Poverty   66
FIGURE 4.8   Demonstration of Economic Growth,
              1989–2005   68
FIGURE 4.9   TFP's Contribution for China and India,
              1989–2005   70
FIGURE 4.10   TFP's Contribution for East Asian Tigers,
              1989–2005   71
FIGURE 4.11   PISA Achievement Scores, 2003   73
FIGURE 4.12   PISA Science Scores, 2006   74
FIGURE 4.13   PISA Mathematics Scores, 2006   75

FIGURE 6.1   BAU and Stabilisation Trajectories for
              450–550ppm CO_2e   124
FIGURE 6.2   Reducing Emissions Requires Action
              Across Many Sectors   126

FIGURE 6.3   Levelised Costs of Different Technologies
              (£/MWh): Carbon Price €40 per tonne CO_2 133
FIGURE 6.4   Cost of Electricity for Different
              Technologies   134
FIGURE 6.5   Public Energy R&D Investments as a
              Share of GDP   135
FIGURE 6.6   Per Capita CO_2 Emissions (in tonnes)   140

THE CONTRIBUTORS

Lee Hsien Loong is Singapore's third Prime Minister. He is also Chairman of the Research, Innovation and Enterprise Council, an international panel to oversee Singapore's major effort in promoting R&D. He launched policies to build a competitive economy and an inclusive society. He has held Ministerial portfolios in Trade and Industry, Defence, Finance, and was Chairman of the Monetary Authority of Singapore. He also served as Deputy Prime Minister with responsibilities for economic and civil service matters. Before entering politics, he was Brigadier-General in the Singapore Armed Forces. He studied at the University of Cambridge, graduating with a Degree in Mathematics and a Diploma in Computer Science. He also obtained a Masters in Public Administration from the Kennedy School of Government, Harvard University.

Saw Swee-Hock is Professorial Fellow at the Institute of Southeast Asian Studies, Singapore and Honorary Professor in the University of Hong Kong and Xiamen University. He was the founding Professor of Statistics at the University of Hong Kong and the National University of Singapore. He is an Honorary Fellow of the London School of Economics and Political Science. His publications are mainly on statistics, demography and finance.

Mustafa Izzuddin is a Ph.D. candidate in the Department of International Relations at the London School of Economics and Political Science. He was a former Research Associate at the Institute of Southeast Asian Studies, Singapore.

Danny Quah is the Head of Department and Professor of Economics at the London School of Economics and Political Science. He is also a Research Fellow at the Centre for Economic Policy Research in London, a Governor of the National Institute of Economic and Social Research, and on the Editorial Board of the *Journal of Economic Growth*. He has also served on the Academic Panels of HM Treasury and the Office of National Statistics. He was a former Assistant Professor in the Department of Economics at the Massachusetts Institute of Technology.

Conor Gearty is Professor of Human Rights Law and the first Rausing Director of the Centre for the Study of Human Rights at the London School of Economics and Political Science. He is also a legal correspondent for *The Tablet* and founding member of Matrix Chambers. He was a former Professor at King's College London.

Nikolas Rose is James Martin Professor of Sociology and Director of the BIOS Centre for the Study of Bioscience, Biotechnology and Society at the London School of Economics and Political Science. He is also a member of the Nuffield Council on Bioethics, and Chair of the Advisory Board of the ESRC Centre for Research on Economic and Socio-Cultural Change. He was a former Managing Editor of *Economy and Society* and is currently a co-editor of *BioSocieties*, an interdisciplinary journal for social studies of the life sciences.

Nicholas Stern is IG Patel Professor of Economics and Government and Director of the Asia Research Centre and of the India Observatory at the London School of Economics and Political Science. Before this, he was adviser to the U.K. Government on the Economics of Climate Change and Development, Head of the Stern Review on the Economics of Climate Change, Head of the U.K. Government Economic Service, Second Permanent Secretary of Her Majesty's Treasury, Director of Policy and Research for the Prime Minister's Commission for Africa, and Chief Economist and Senior Vice President at the World Bank. He was instrumental in the setting up of the LSE Asia Research Centre.

John T. Sidel is Sir Patrick Gillam Professor of International and Comparative Politics at the London School of Economics and Political Science. He is a specialist on Southeast Asia, with a special focus on the Philippines and Indonesia. He was formerly a Reader in Southeast Asian Politics at the School of Oriental and African Studies, University of London.

PREFACE

The London School of Economics and Political Science has been organising the LSE Asia Forum in different parts of Asia, with the first one held in Bangkok in March 2004, the second in Hong Kong in September 2005, and the third in New Delhi in December 2006. The LSE Asia Forum 2008 was jointly organized with the Institute of Southeast Asian Studies in April 2008 in Singapore, with *The Politics of Knowledge* as the theme of the forum.

It was decided in the early planning stage that, unlike the previous three forums, the proceedings of the 2008 Forum should be published in a book under the joint imprint of LSE and ISEAS. The actual publication would be handled by ISEAS Publishing. Except for Chapter 2 which was specifically written after the Forum for inclusion in the book, the other six chapters are the revised version of the papers presented in the Forum. The book serves as a permanent record of the important event held in Singapore as well as a valuable contribution to the discourse on the politics of knowledge that is playing a pivotal role in shaping the economic and social advancement of many regions in our globalising world.

We would like to put on record our grateful thanks to the distinguished speakers who have taken their valuable time to speak at the Forum as well as revising their papers for publication. Our thanks go to Howard Davies, Director of LSE, and Ambassador

K. Kesavapany, Director of ISEAS, for their encouragement and support in the organisation of the Forum and the publication of this book, and Mrs Triena Ong, Managing Editor, for overseeing the publication aspects. We must of course thank the many sponsors whose generous donations have contributed to the immediate success of the Forum and to the happy outcome as represented by this book. Finally, the views expressed in the book are those of the contributors and do not necessarily represent those of the institutions they represent.

Saw Swee-Hock and Danny Quah
September 2008

FOREWORD

This book is the outcome of the fourth LSE Asia Forum which the Institute of Southeast Asian Studies (ISEAS) co-hosted in Singapore on 11 April 2008. Global trends as well as more recent developments in the domestic politics of regional countries have made a forum on the politics of knowledge most timely.

As much as we will need to deepen our knowledge of politics, the politics of knowledge aided and abetted by the ceaseless changes in information technology will increasingly be part of the wider political contestations of our times. Whether all this will have liberating, democratizing and enfranchising effects on peoples and societies remains to be fully explored. To some, knowledge may not necessarily bring with it power — instead a sense of powerlessness.

Sustained economic growth can be attributed to good governance and openness to trade but undoubtedly too, knowledge and technology meld into a powerful driver of growth as evidenced by the success of the East Asian economies particularly China's. At the same time the commercialization of scientific knowledge can also lead to multiple conflicts between commercial interests and perceptions of the common good. Such conflicts need to be addressed, managed and governed. In modern society, access to and delivery of knowledge — in pursuit of "the truth" — is often subordinated to political contest. Does the

Asian condition and "Asian values" provide any contextualization to the right of free speech in furtherance of the truth? New avenues to the dissemination of knowledge have in Asia and elsewhere created new opportunities for those who seek to pose challenges within established structures of religious knowledge and authority. Finally with respect to the pressing problems of our times posed by climate change and environmental degradation not just to Asia but to mankind as a whole, the need for sound analysis, understanding and knowledge culled from many disciplines is a crucial underpin to informed policy making.

The quest for knowledge will never cease as long as mankind thinks, continues to be curious and constantly seeks innovation, adaptation and progress. Just as the chapters of this book stem from a growing awareness of the sociological, economic, political and legal implications of an ever widening frontier of current knowledge, it will I am sure, also inspire other enquiries into and discourses on the subject of knowledge-making for some time to come. We in Singapore are also deeply engaged in building both a knowledge- and science-based economy as well as hopefully a more cultured society along the way. Such aspirations demand heavy investments in research and development and the establishment of institutes and think-tanks such as ISEAS. Other ASEAN countries in their surge up the developmental ladder will also be increasingly attracted to the potentials and promise of a knowledge economy. The issues raised in this book re-awaken us to the need to rise to the challenge as well as tap into the new opportunities opening up along the frontiers of new knowledge through appropriate and enlightened policies.

K. Kesavapany
Director
Institute of Southeast Asian Studies

MESSAGES

Unlike the previous three Forums organized by the LSE in Bangkok, Hong Kong and New Delhi, the LSE Asia Forum 2008 on "The Politics of Knowledge" held in Singapore was the first to be jointly organized with a local institution as represented by the Institute of Southeast Asian Studies (ISEAS).

Another first was the publication of the papers presented in the Forum in a book to provide a permanent record to a wider audience. Those fortunate enough to attend the Forum were treated to stimulating presentations by the distinguished panel of speakers and discussants. I am delighted that ISEAS has been able to contribute to the success of the Forum and the publication of this book during the year of ISEAS' 40th Anniversary.

Wang Gungwu
Chairman, ISEAS Board of Trustees

The LSE strives to achieve the highest academic standards in teaching and research in the social sciences. It also aims to contribute knowledge for the common good, to a global audience of governments, other policymakers, international business, multilateral institutions and the informed general public. This volume was created from the knowledge delivered to a large audience at the latest LSE Asia Forum held in Singapore on 11 April 2008. I hope that you find it a valuable contribution to some of the most pressing public policy issues of our day.

Peter Sutherland
Chairman, LSE Board of Governors

Chapter 1

ROLE OF KNOWLEDGE IN THE TRANSFORMATION OF ASIA

Lee Hsien Loong

INTRODUCTION

I am happy to join you this morning at this LSE Asia Forum. LSE has always had a strong Singapore connection. For decades, it has attracted top Singapore students studying in the UK. Many have left their mark in a wide range of professions. Several have distinguished themselves in public service. Two LSE alumni have served in the Cabinet so far — Dr Goh Keng Swee, who was our first Finance Minister (and much more besides), and Mr Tharman Shanmugaratnam, the current Finance Minister. It is an illustrious record.

KNOWLEDGE ECONOMIES IN ASIA

The theme of this conference — knowledge — engages many of us in Asia. The whole continent is on the move today, because China and India have taken off. But Asian countries know that to sustain their growth and improve their people's lives, the use and creation of knowledge are crucial. Hence many countries are seeking to educate their people, upgrade their economies, and create conditions for knowledge and innovation to flourish.

Knowledge creation is not a new phenomenon in Asia. The ancient Indian civilisation made significant contributions at the frontiers of knowledge. Fundamental mathematical concepts like the number zero and the decimal system, as well as inventions like rocket artillery and coins, can be traced back to India.

Ancient China was arguably the most technologically advanced society in the world. This pre-eminent status lasted for at least two thousand years until around the 15th century. The monumental efforts of Joseph Needham and others to document China's scientific history reveal the long list of its discoveries and inventions: the magnetic compass, gun-powder, paper, printing, and porcelain, to name just a few, were all available in China centuries before they became known in the West.

However, China did not realise the full potential of the ingenuity and inventiveness of its people, and the scientific knowledge that it had accumulated over the centuries. Instead under the Ming and Qing dynasties China closed itself to the outside world. Chinese society stagnated, and eventually decayed and broke down. In contrast, Europe from the 16th century onwards saw dramatic advances and breakthroughs, as scientists like Copernicus, Galileo and Newton revolutionised scientific thinking and laid the foundations of modern science. This set the stage for the intellectual movement of the Enlightenment, and later the Industrial Revolution, and today's modern developed economies.

Today Asia continues to lag behind the West in the level of science, engineering, technology, all key fields of knowledge for economic development and human progress. But this is changing with schools, colleges, universities and research institutes sprouting across China and at a more measured pace also in India.

Both China and India have deep talent pools, with huge numbers of extremely able and bright people. This talent has scattered all round the world, and are making themselves felt in top universities in the U.S. and U.K., in the City of London and Silicon Valley. Top Chinese and Indian universities like Beijing University and the Indian Institute of Technology (IIT) have student bodies which are collectively at least as bright as the top universities in the West. Statistically, their admissions are indeed more competitive. Indian students are known to apply to IIT first, and only if they fail, go to MIT.

However, what the universities in China and India have not yet succeeded in doing is to create the environment of open inquiry and experimentation, conducive to, and indeed essential for, cutting-edge research and major breakthroughs. Researchers in these countries have yet to win Nobel Prizes in the sciences, or Fields Medals in mathematics, although Chinese and Indian scientists and mathematicians working abroad have done so. One reason is that these universities have a less diverse academic community. Unlike the top Western universities, they do not draw the best students, researchers and professors from around the world. The intellectual ferment and exchange required to challenge great minds to do great things is not yet there. They are also weighed down by the legacy of academic hierarchies based on seniority rather than talent, unlike the best American universities. This is changing, but it will take time. Meanwhile we already see more researchers from Chinese and Indian institutions publishing papers in leading international academic journals.

The growing scientific and technological prowess of China and India is an important factor in their economic takeoff. India was not long ago seen as the world's back office for low-end business process outsourcing (BPO), but it is now doing more and more knowledge-intensive work, like interpretation of medical scans, data mining and modelling, and writing of legal briefs. Indian BPO companies like Infosys, Wipro and Tata are all providing high value-added, complex systems solutions to MNCs around the world. Their operations are as sophisticated and knowledge-intensive as global companies like Google or Accenture.

Similarly, China is not just growing low-end industries, but making rapid in-roads into high-tech sectors. MNCs are setting up not just manufacturing plants in China, but also R&D centres to take advantage of the abundant supply of talented Chinese engineers. We are starting to see home-grown Chinese high-tech firms like Huawei and Lenovo, which design new products using indigenous technology. Having established themselves in the domestic market, they are now expanding abroad, and competing in the global league.

In Southeast Asia too, countries are striving to upgrade through education and technology. Malaysia, which decided to use Malay to teach all subjects in state schools a generation ago, has now switched back to using English to teach mathematics and science. This switch has not been easy, either politically or practically. But the Malaysian Government has committed to this reform because it understands that this is the only way to keep in touch with developments in the world, and give their population the best chance of keeping up in a global knowledge economy.

Vietnam, which is on the verge of economic take-off, is also emphasising education. Vietnamese students are highly motivated and quick to learn. They have an aptitude for science and mathematics, and consistently excel in international Olympiads. Vietnamese workers also show tremendous drive to improve themselves. Huge numbers take classes after work to learn English, and many now want to learn Chinese. They know that English will open doors to a world of knowledge and technology, and Chinese will expand economic opportunities.

SINGAPORE'S APPROACH

As a small country with no natural resources, Singapore has long known that we have no choice but to make the mastery of knowledge our competitive advantage. We have been implicitly building a knowledge economy, long before this became a buzzword. From the late 70s, we realised we could not differentiate ourselves from our competitors or raise our standards of living by competing on cost alone. Hence we pursued several strategies to build up this knowledge edge.

First, we have invested heavily in our people through education. Our aim is to give every child a top-rate education, and invest in where his aptitudes lie. Therefore our emphasis is on the quality of all our schools, and not just a few elite schools. The goal is to teach students how to think, to be creative in problem-solving, and to keep on absorbing new knowledge and skills all their life, rather than to squeeze more facts and data into an already full curriculum. Hence our slogan: "Teach Less Learn More".

We acknowledge that not every student has the same ability and talent. So we are creating diverse and flexible options for students to choose a path which suits them, instead of trying to cast everyone within a few moulds. Beyond the schools, our junior colleges prepare students for university education, both locally and abroad; our polytechnics impart professional expertise through a practice-based curriculum; and our Institute of Technical Education equips students with hands-on technical skills and critical thinking habits. These heavy investments in human capital, across the whole spectrum of skills, are equipping our people to compete a knowledge economy.

Second, we have encouraged the free flow of information. This is the way to keep ourselves fully abreast of new developments and ideas, and to be ready to react promptly to a changing world. Singapore is fully plugged into the world, and wide open to the cross-currents of global interactions. Because English has been our working language, it gave us a tremendous advantage in the Internet age. As an air and sea hub, we are linked up physically to the rest of the world, and as a telecommunications hub we are fully hooked up, whether wired or wireless, whether through the Internet or cable TV. We still need to filter the flow of information, to maintain basic standards of decency, and preserve racial and religious harmony, but it is confined to a very minimum. All this is essential to nurture knowledge industries, whether it is financial services, interactive and digital media, or just-in-time manufacturing.

Third, we are stepping up our R&D efforts, from basic R&D to translational research to development work close to the end products and markets. We are setting up research centres and programmes in our universities, to study focussed areas where our modest efforts can make an impact, like cancers and infectious diseases that are common in Asia, and natural disasters and climate change in our region. We are creating an integrated environment for collaboration across disciplines and institutions, thus maximising opportunities for cross-fertilisation of ideas and expertise. Through such cross-disciplinary efforts, we aim to be part of the global endeavour to push out the new frontiers of knowledge and possibilities.

Fourth, the whole tenor of our society is geared towards welcoming new ideas, and adapting to change. Our ethos is cosmopolitan and pragmatic. Our society is meritocratic and egalitarian — everyone has a chance to learn and excel. We strive to operate rationally and flexibly, and to keep our sense of identity as an Asian society without being constrained by rigid social hierarchy or stifling political correctness. We respect the rule of law and intellectual property rights. We reward effort and work, encourage risk-taking, and embrace diversity.

This broader social and political context helps us to create an environment which attracts talent and entrepreneurs from around the world. They come because here they can access information, markets and global services, operate within a reliable, efficient and honest business environment, and do well for themselves and thus for Singapore. They bring with them diverse experiences, extensive expertise and new ideas, which add to the richness of our society and spur our own people to innovate and break new ground.

CHALLENGES AHEAD

To stay competitive on the global stage, Asian countries have to keep on moving in this direction of knowledge, scientific excellence and innovation. But it will not always be a smooth journey. There will be difficulties to overcome along the way. Let me highlight three broad challenges.

The first challenge is to ensure that everyone in a society benefits from the knowledge economy. Even as we strive to develop every individual's abilities and talents, we know that those without the right skills will have an increasingly difficult time. The premium on ability and skill is high and growing. IT is automating simple jobs. We already see automated checkout lines at supermarkets and touch-screen check-in kiosks at airports. In the coming decades, many more routine jobs will be replaced by computers or robots that work 24/7, and cost less than the wages that a worker will expect. Overall the knowledge economy will be a boon for mankind, but individual workers will need the skills to do things which the computers and robotic tools cannot do.

This is why we in Singapore are investing heavily in continuous education and training, to help vulnerable workers learn new skills, and master new jobs. It is also why we are emphasising quality education for all, and paying special attention to children from low-income families, so that we reduce the problem of poverty in the next generation.

Another challenge is the complete and instant exposure to an over-whelming torrent of information through the Internet and online channels. This brings great economic benefits, and great potential for sharing and using knowledge, but it also causes people to respond to unfiltered, raw information or misinformation without the benefit of reflection time or informed interpretation. Furthermore, instant communication is not just about conveying information. Inflammatory opinions, half-truths and untruths will also gain currency through viral distribution. The online film "Fitna" which has offended Muslims worldwide is just the latest example of wrong-headedness, asserting the right to freedom of expression in democratic Holland while overlooking the costs, namely the stoking of hatred between devout Muslims and Christians. Terrorist groups are using the Internet too, to find recruits, spread their extremist ideologies, and prepare attacks.

With satellite TV and the Internet, events are also magnified across a global listening board. The world is now their stage. We see this in the protests that have erupted during the Olympic torch relay. The Olympics is China's coming out party, to celebrate its progress and opening up to the world. They sent the Olympic torch overseas in what is described as a "journey of harmony".

But not surprisingly, China's opponents see this as a golden opportunity to make their point. So as the torch travels the world, it has faced challenges at virtually every stop so far. Vivid TV images of demonstrators waving banners, scuffling with police, and making concerted assaults to snuff out the flame are beamed live around the world, achieving an asymmetrical prominence, and so influencing public opinion against China and the Games.

No protesting group truly expects that their public display of anger and outrage at China's treatment of Tibetans or ethnic Han dissidents will change China's policy when it affects its core security concerns. They know no government can give ground on any core issue under such public duress, whatever the merits of the arguments. So whatever the intentions of the demonstrators, the people of China believe they want to inflict maximum humiliation on China and the Chinese people more than the Chinese Government. The outrage in China, especially among the young, can be read on the flooded Internet bulletin boards, all carrying virulent anti-foreign sentiments. Pity they are in unintelligible Chinese ideographs. Were they in the English language, young Americans and Europeans would realise that these displays of contempt for China and things Chinese will have consequences in their lifetime, well beyond the Olympic Games.

In this new environment of raw, unprocessed information with instant worldwide impact, it will not be easy to keep the public debate on a high plane, especially on controversial issues where emotions rather than reason prevail. This will change the texture of societies everywhere. Societies will have to adapt and evolve defensive mechanisms and habits to thrive in these new circumstances. Amidst unceasing and bewildering changes, we will all the more need strong moral and social values that help us keep our bearings and hold our societies together.

Finally, fostering a sense of national identity will be a major challenge, especially for small and open societies like Singapore. Globalisation and the knowledge economy have created a single worldwide market for talent. In every field, the most able people are in demand worldwide, and are also highly mobile. The best musicians and sportspersons are already a global breed. But to do well, a country needs a core of its ablest citizens, those with both the intellectual and social acumen, to play leadership roles in the economy, the administration, and the political leadership. Without that central core to take the country forward, the society cannot perform to its full potential, and the citizens will suffer.

Big countries like China and India can sustain large outflows of top talent over years or decades, and still be able to retain a central core. Smaller countries like Singapore risk being depleted much faster. More and more Singaporeans are going abroad, whether to study or work. We must accept this flow as a reality, and bring in talent to top up, and encourage Singaporeans who study and work abroad to eventually return and add to the vibrancy of their own society. We will need not only to create economic opportunities here, but also opportunities for people to develop their potential and express their human spirit. Ultimately we must create an emotional attachment to the country, their family members, school and college mates, buddies in National Service platoons, and friends, both to hold our own people and to get others to strike roots here. Then we can maintain our own identity and sense of common destiny. Then we will have the conviction and the sense of purpose to sustain what we have built, and bring it to ever greater heights.

CONCLUSION

Despite these challenges, Asia's transformation will continue. It will be powered by knowledge and ideas, and by billions of increasingly-skilled workers and entrepreneurs continually searching for new and better ways of doing things. The politics in Asian countries will inevitably change, too. The outcome will not be determined by pressure from outside, but by the internal processes in these countries, which are old societies with deep cultures and long histories.

Not all Asian countries will effortlessly adapt to this new environment. But all will make the effort, several will excel, and many will eventually make the grade. Singapore will try its best to be among those who will succeed.

Chapter 2

UNDERSTANDING THE POLITICS OF KNOWLEDGE
The Asian Perspective
Saw Swee-Hock and Mustafa Izzuddin

Knowledge is Power is today a commonplace in an increasingly globalised world in which there is a much greater and renewed emphasis on the creation of an information economy, a knowledge-based economy or a knowledge society.[1] Echoing this sentiment in his address at the LSE Asia Forum 2008, Singapore's Prime Minister Lee Hsien Loong (thereafter, Premier Lee) underscored the importance of creating favourable conditions for knowledge and innovation to flourish so that Asian countries can sustain their economic growth and improve their people's lives. It is an active engagement and interaction with knowledge and technology that has the whole Asian continent on the move today with China and India having economically taken off in such dramatic fashion. Similarly, more and more writers such as Kishore Mahbubani have also begun to argue that there is an *irresistible shift of global power to the East* from the standpoint that Asians have finally understood, absorbed and implemented

Western best practices in many areas while also being innovative in their own way by creating new patterns of cooperation not seen in the West. Asians are thus ready to move from being bystanders in world history to becoming co-drivers in foreign policy matters including the quest for knowledge and technology.[2]

Premier Lee also argued that knowledge creation is not a new phenomenon in Asia. He illustrated with examples that both the ancient Indian and ancient Chinese civilisations made significant contributions to the frontiers of knowledge — new knowledge was discovered and developed centuries before they became known to the West. Even the early Southeast Asian civilisations of Cambodia (Angkorian period) and Java (Srivijayan period) were the results of knowledge and a complex Hindu culture. Lest we forget that the Great Islamic Civilisation was also the result of the quest and acquisition of all kinds of knowledge besides those relating to religion, and many have argued that our civilisation today began with the European quest of knowledge from the Muslim Arabs and other Muslim races, and the West of course had a head start in the Industrial Age.

Against the backdrop of the rise and domination of Western civilisation and its attendant colonial and imperialist tendencies, the notion of the politics of knowledge became clearly visible. It remains visible today as accurately observed by Premier Lee that Asia continues to lag behind the West in the level of science, engineering, technology and all key fields of knowledge for economic development and human progress. To talk about the politics of knowledge is to talk about knowledge as being a form of controlled resource: knowledge is an exercise of power and that knowledge itself produces power. This power-knowledge relationship is derived from and is influenced by Michel Foucault whose works have been viewed as essentially social constructionist (knowledge is socially constructed, being influenced by language and discourse) in a postmodern mode.³ Central to Foucault's work is the idea that all power requires knowledge and all knowledge relies on and reinforces existing power relations. Hence, there is no such thing as "truth" existing outside of power. Foucault's work is important when one speaks of a knowledge-based economy since such an economy is often influenced by power, and those states which have privileged sources of power control knowledge. Framing it in the Orientalist context in his seminal work on Orientalism, Edward Said similarly argues that because of the politics of identity, that is, exclusion of "others" (Orientals) from the "self" (West), the politics of knowledge involves the separation and exclusion of knowledge, with knowledge being the sole preserve of the West.⁴

In understanding this prevailing politics of knowledge, the LSE Asia Forum 2008 addresses the challenging issues facing Asian governments, policy-makers, businesspeople, and others in supporting and promoting the growth of knowledge-based economics against the backdrop of long-standing Western monopoly (Euro-centrism) and Asia's current renaissance with the emergence of China and India as key partners in managing the dynamics of globalisation and growth in the region and beyond. In covering four main sub-themes — knowledge as driver of economic growth, protecting knowledge, controlling knowledge and sharing knowledge — this Forum also explores the strategic and policy developments in Asia and in particular, the implications and prospects for Asia by understanding the politics of knowledge. It details out approaches suitable for Asian nations that are more or less likely to differ from those adopted in the West.

In line with the first sub-theme of the Forum "Knowledge as a Driver for Economic Growth" which seeks to explore the production of knowledge, and its value as an economic driver,

Danny Quah's chapter examines, rather boldly, how a decade after those tumultuous events of the 1997 Asian Financial Crisis (AFC), Emerging Asia has surprised many with the post-1997 Asian reality turning out to be largely a success thus disproving downhearted expectations just a decade ago. Quah contends that emerging Asia has been freshly restored as the world's economic powerhouse even after the major East Asian economies were perceived as catastrophes of financial excesses, corporate and political misgovernance, and diminishing returns to over-investment during the 1997 AFC. Based on the recent successes exhibited by emerging Asia along multiple dimensions, Quah unequivocally believes that "the world's economic centre of gravity [will] continue to shift east".

Quah points out that one such recent success was that the economic strength in Emerging Asia has lifted hundreds of millions of people out of extreme poverty, which is a striking achievement not experienced in the world in the last quarter of a century. China alone had alleviated extreme poverty for half a billion of its citizens. Quah also notes that a second success was that although still relatively small in size, Emerging Asia's contribution to the global economic growth was equally comparable to that of the G7 economies (excluding Japan for argument purposes) which are many times larger. He argues that contrary to popular belief, Emerging Asian economic growth has accelerated and gotten even stronger after 1997 so much so that "it is as if 1997 was just an irrelevance". Even at market exchange rates, Quah postulates that China and India when combined contributes just as much as the United States of America does to world economic growth.

Overall, Quah evinces that this eastward economic shift has been brought about by sustained economic growth, the fundamentals of which include good governance and openness to trade as well as creativity and innovation in economic processes: knowledge and technology. For the latter, Quah asserts that the Emerging Asian economies, especially the ones in East Asia, have achieved higher standards of performance particularly in information and communications technology (ICT) when compared to the G7 economies. While these recent successes are striking, Quah revealed that there are also some within Emerging Asia that have fallen behind and also emphasised the need to improve in schooling and education more broadly — as also accentuated by Premier Lee in calling for the universities in China and India to further diversify its academic community and "create the environment of open inquiry and experimentation, conducive to, and indeed essential for, cutting-edge research and major breakthroughs". But both Premier Lee and Quah maintained that despite these challenges, there is a noticeable eastward shift to Emerging Asia in this information age.

Based on the second sub-theme of the Forum "Protecting Knowledge: balancing commercial needs and public benefits" which seeks to examine issues surrounding the protection of knowledge and in particular, looking at the conflict between the commercial need to protect and restrict the use of knowledge, and the social need to provide greater access, Nikolas Rose explores the conflicts over the commercialisation of biomedical (scientific) knowledge (commerce versus the common good) while Conor Gearty discusses the "unique contribution of human rights to the growth of a relative approach to knowledge which nevertheless requires for its effectiveness a commitment to one absolute, or near absolute, notably the principle of free speech".

Taking the example of Singapore where the bioeconomy is viewed as a crucial economic driver, Rose observes that governments across Asia and beyond have also followed a similar path in pushing for breakthroughs in biomedical research with the primary aim of enhancing economic competitiveness and achieving scientific prestige in this age of "translational medicine" (belief that there is a crucial link between advances in basic biological knowledge of human biology and the understanding and effective treatment of different types of diseases). Rose's candid observation of Singapore's push to become "Asia's biotech tiger" in fact coincides with Premier Lee's illustration of Singapore's approach to step up research and development (and cross-disciplinary) efforts so that the country remains "part of the global endeavour to push out the new frontiers of knowledge and possibilities". Premier Lee also advised Asian countries to keep progressing in the "direction of knowledge, scientific excellence and innovation" so as to stay competitive on the global stage.

Rose adds that the belief in "translational medicine" and its link-up with regulators, researchers, clinicians, politicians and actual and potential patients has come to constitute a "political economy of hope". Consequently, Rose contends that it is the link between health and wealth and between virtue and profit that drives the expanding "biomedical bioeconomy" across Asia and beyond but at the same time this "knowledge-based bioeconomy" also generates conflicts between health and wealth and between commerce and the commons, which has to be managed and governed so that the trust in scientific (biomedical) knowledge is legitimately regained in a global and unjust world.

One such conflict, according to Rose, is that while patents provide protection for invention, they can limit competition since it encourages a climate of secrecy which engenders the hindrance of a free flow of ideas on which scientific progress relies upon. He argues, as many others do, that "the principles that should govern scientific knowledge were being compromised by the drive for intellectual property [patenting] and the growing entanglements between universities, researchers, industry and knowledge claims". Focusing on gene patenting and its attendant difficulties in the "ownership of genes", Rose enumerates the concerns and effects of such patents on scientific knowledge. One such concern is "the right of sources", which asserts that as genetic information derives from a source (individual or group), that source "should retain some rights in it or in the profits made from it".[5] The second concern is of anti-commons where "the patenting of a gene sequence may hamper or even prevent others from working on it even when the owner does not consider it worth pursuing, thus blocking potential lines of discovery." The third concern is the disputable "patenting of a gene sequence with a test to identify disease-related variants" in which case genomic information on disease risk is not viewed as a public good. The final concern is that "patenting leads to a rush to translation" whereby "patenting gives an incentive to commercialise the discovery and take the product to the market in order to recoup the initial costs of the research and to generate profit before the patent expires, irrespective of wider social concerns".

Rose's revelation of some of the "general downsides of the dependence of drug development and production on commercial corporations [i.e. pharmaceuticals] and market mechanisms" is of worthy mention. First is the issue of evidence and efficacy whereby in virtually all the regions in the world, "drugs can only be licensed if they meet certain conditions set by regulatory bodies" and "commercial pressures to bring the drug through the licensing system generate many problems". Second is the issue of selective reporting where "companies are not legally required to submit evidence from all trials they have conducted, and many trials that give ambiguous or negative results are not published, skewing risk-benefit calculations". Third is the issue of publication bias which points to the fact that "drug trials published in scientific journals that have been carried out or funded by pharmaceutical companies report higher levels of efficacy and lower levels of unwanted effects and adverse incidents than those carried out by independent researchers". Fourth is the issue of corporate capture which points to the "actual and perceived conflicts where universities or departments have more general financial links with biotech companies, either in the form of gifts or more specific arrangements". Fifth is the self-explanatory conflict of interests between those who sit on regulatory bodies and having financial links with pharmaceutical companies. The final issue is that of the outsourcing of trials which means that numerous drug trials are undertaken by pharmaceutical companies in less developed regions since it is certainly far cheaper to do so.

Overall, Rose decisively concludes that the "drive to patent and to commercialise leads to priority being given to the development of those products that will meet the demands of those who have both the willingness and ability to pay" and in the broader scheme of things, this would invariably result in the conflicts over the commercialisation of biomedical (scientific) knowledge which in many respects is classified as a common (public) good.

In his chapter, Gearty accentuates that one's understanding of knowledge underpins one's attitude to free speech. He further suggests that knowledge is seen as something created out of one's intercommunications rather than simply discovered or received as "tablets of stones from some higher authority". This is consonant with Foucault's thesis that knowledge is not found but rather produced through languages and practices (discourses) which then makes knowledge significant. But this raises the issue of the politics behind the understanding of knowledge in which Gearty asks: whose version of the truth is to be heard, and which version of the truth prevails? Foucault's concept of power-knowledge hits home this point when he argues (in broad terms) that while power is based on knowledge and utilises knowledge, it also reproduces knowledge on its own terms, and this is where the version of the truth becomes disputable and as Foucault would argue, there is no truth outside discourses. Subsequently, Gearty posits the argument that free speech is a vital guarantor of freedom that only democratic forms of government can deliver, and through which the flourishing of all (including the poor and dispossessed) can be best secured. He adds that neither human rights nor free speech is a hangover of colonialism — it is in fact a key ingredient in the successful effort that every society must make to face the future.

In the first half of his chapter, Gearty restates and defends the universality of human rights particularly against relativist claims which asserts that "the very idea is itself a creature of colonial or imperial power". Gearty advises his readers to reject the idea of human rights being inherently a Western construct that is to say, being the possession of the West or "Global North" because this is a profoundly wrong perspective. To substantiate this, he analyses the arguments of the sceptics of universalism, and explains why their assertions are in fact more appearance than reality. By the same token, Gearty also demonstrates that far from being a challenge to local values, human rights (including prioritising free speech) in a way represents a vindication of the best of these values.

Gearty highlights the widely-held belief that the development of the human rights discourse is tied up with the story of the West — emphasising the nexus between cultural specificity and human rights. It is also quite clear, according to Gearty, that the idea of human rights (including free speech) has been central to the democratising and thus to the ethical foundations of many new national powers in years gone by. Put another way, Gearty recognises that the very prominence of human rights over the past sixty years (post-World War II) has stemmed from its value to the great powers and particularly American power. However, Gearty reveals that the sceptical direction that thought has taken in the West has shaken the confidence in truth upon which the idea of human rights have depended upon, and which has thus implications on the universality debate: if human rights no longer hold "true" for the North, how can they be "true" for the rest of the world? To overcome this conundrum, Gearty intimates that the human rights discourse emphasises a more localised narrative with foundations less rooted in the work of European thinkers of the past. Gearty argues that the delocalisation of the idea of human rights involves the peeling away of several culturally-specific layers that have become widely regarded as largely irrelevant. This also meant the realisation of human rights not as rights as such but as values that underpin these rights such as the respect for human dignity, liberty and autonomy of the individual and the principle of representative government according to law. Equally important is that free speech principles suffuses through all of these values, and there is a renewed emphasis on the virtue of tolerance and a commitment to diversity. This has become the beauty and strength of the human rights discourse.

In the second half of his chapter, Gearty further explores the universal meaning of human rights by evaluating the Asian values debate which has been a key fixture of human rights discourse in the past twenty years. Encapsulated in the 1993 Bangkok Declaration in preparation for the World Conference on Human Rights in Vienna the same year, the Asian Values appeared to threaten the universality of human rights by suggesting that "respect for human rights (and free speech) was little more than a provincial piece of Western thinking for which the rest of the world should have no sensible use". Gearty suggests that the human rights idea has come out stronger from its intellectual joust with 'Asian values' in which case it is better able to frame the right responses to cultural critiques, and abandon baggage from the past that does not dovetail with the human rights discourse today. Gearty creatively surmises that the Asian values critique has a hand in making the human rights subject a "fitter and leaner intellectual, political and activist beast".

Gearty concludes by reiterating that while the meaning of the term 'human rights' may have changed over time, in its essentials, it still stands for a view on human behaviour that is the exclusive preserve of no single culture or peoples. It is a universalist human rights discourse in which no particular culture or code of laws has superiority, but is committed to the avoidance of cruelty on one hand and to personal growth (open society with free speech) on the other. Gearty balances her argument by revealing that the commitment to free speech as a source of political knowledge (free speech influenced by power) involves a critique of not only of non-democratic or partly democratic states but also of well-entrenched democratic nations which are just as guilty of controlling free speech in ways that appear at odds with the human rights discourse.

Gearty also points out that the proponents of human rights acknowledge that free speech cannot be unrestrained and that such a discourse does not occur in a vacuum in which politics do not operate. The journey of the Olympics torch across the world en route to Beijing for the 2008 Olympic Games is a case in point. Rather than this event being seen as a "journey of harmony", both Gearty and Premier Lee concurred that this gave an unfortunate opportunity for China's opponents to zero in on China's violation of human rights with regard to the treatment of the Tibetans and ethnic Han dissidents. Overall, Gearty recognises that there are limitations to the human rights discourse, and that is why the universalist argument appears more cogent and seemingly holds greater currency.

In line with the third sub-theme of the Forum "Controlling Knowledge: responding to contest and change in control over religious knowledge" which seeks to explore the control of knowledge by focusing specifically on the use of religious knowledge both as a means of transfer of ideas and information and as a means of control and censorship of knowledge, John Sidel studies the changing politics of religious knowledge in Asia by taking Indonesia as his case study. Sidel contends that although little appears to have changed in terms of the broad structures of political power in most Asian countries, the established structures of religious knowledge and authority have come to face new challenges and new rival claimants as well. Sidel adds that even in this profane world of Asian politics in which repression and authoritarian rule is commonplace, it is not unusual to speak of tectonic shifts in the politics of religious knowledge or the democratisation of religion due to the expanding exercise of effective religious freedoms over the past two decades.

Sidel further explains that thanks to urbanisation and increasing access to ICT, more and more Asians today "enjoy greater freedom to acquire religious knowledge, greater access to diverse sources of religious knowledge and greater capacity to acquire, accumulate, and actively enjoy and articulate religious knowledge themselves". As a consequence, there is a democratisation of religion in Asia in which the steep hierarchies of religious authority are increasingly challenged, and contested by rival sources and sites of religious knowledge, and in which greater freedom of choice, of exit, and of voice is ever more evident in this changing religious landscape in Asia.

Sidel proceeds to explain that the pattern of religious democratisation is evident in Asia in at least three ways. First is that economic, social and political change has reduced some of the formal and informal restrictions upon religious life in parts of Communist Asia. Second is that there has been a proliferation of new sources of religious authority, new claimants to religious knowledge, new arbiters of what it means to know God, and new interpreters of what it means to be a good Buddhist, Christian, Hindu or Muslim. Third is that there are noticeably widening forms of popular participation and the shifting patterns of clerical mediation in religious life in various parts of Asia.

Sidel also affirms that religious democratisation has produced unsettling uncertainties, and is the backdrop by which episodes of violence have taken place in various parts of Asia over the past two decades either in the form of secular state crackdowns on unauthorised religious practices and organisations as evident in China and Vietnam or official religious institutions' efforts to discipline and punish wayward members of their putative flocks as observed in Malaysia. Such violence has also assumed the form of inter-religious conflicts as have been witnessed in India and Indonesia largely because of the twin pressures of democratisation in the realm of politics and heightened uncertainty and flux in the structures of religious authority and identity.

In the case of Indonesia post-Soeharto, Sidel notes that it offers a distinguishable example of the connection between democratisation and inter-religious violence. He postulates that Indonesia "has witnessed a complex pattern of rising and then declining violence in the name of Islam in tandem with the process of [democratic] transition from authoritarian rule over the past decade". This pattern reflected (1) shifts in the structures of religious authority in Indonesia due to the flourishing of diverse forms of religious expression and associational activity such as the rise of new charismatic *kyai* (religious scholars) thanks to the appeal of mystical, Sufistic and 'supernatural' approaches; and (2) a set of uncertainties regarding hierarchies and boundaries of control over the production and circulation of religious knowledge in the country (including the restriction and regulation of women's behaviour in the public realm in accordance with the principles of Islam) by Islamist politicians, parties and organisations amidst the process of political democratisation. It is little wonder then, as Sidel pointedly argues, that the "existing hierarchies of Islamic worship and learning are today facing unprecedented difficulties in maintaining their authority over the diverse population of 200 million Muslims across the archipelago".

That said, when it comes to inter-religious violence and Islamist influence within Indonesia today, Sidel suggests that this has largely subsided within the workings of a consolidated democracy as epitomised by the relative absence of violence in the past several years. This is also greatly due to the observable pattern of accommodation between Muslims and non-Muslims in local politics as evident in the success of GOLKAR and PDIP in the local parliamentary elections and the prevalence of cross-cutting inter-religious coalitions in the elections for local executive posts. Even while Islamist parties like PKS and groups like FPI are popular and do wield influence in local politics, they are seen to exert more informal forms of influence and intimidation in the name of Islam rather than viewed as embarking on a trend of Islamisation in Indonesian state and society.

Overall, Sidel evinces that what one observes in Indonesia, as in Asia, is that efforts to control the production and circulation of religious knowledge has largely failed and that there is fragmentation of religious authority and diversification of religious practices and affiliations accompanying the democratisation, decentralisation and liberalisation of public life. Greater accessibility to ICT has also ushered in religious democratisation because as Premier Lee observes, ICT can "cause people to respond to unfiltered raw information or misinformation without the benefit of reflection time or informed interpretation". Premier Lee presents the example of the online film "Fitna", which while a manifestation of a freedom of expression in democratic Holland, offended Muslims around the world (including Indonesia) and stoked hatred between devout Muslims and Christians. Sidel concedes that there may be limits to the democratisation of religion in the profane world of politics but he affirms that religion will continue to play a key role in the worldly struggles for freedom in Asia and beyond. And in the decades ahead, Sidel reckons that "new forms of religious knowledge will gradually help to create new forms of politics and new constellations of power in Asia as elsewhere in the world". It will be the popular vote that will eventually determine what degree of religious democratisation will prevail in individual Asian states in this profane world of politics.

Based on the final sub-theme of the Forum "Sharing Knowledge: reconciling conflicting aims on climate change and the environment" which seeks to address the problems in creating and using common or shared knowledge to generate regional and international action such as those associated with climate change and the environment, Nicholas Stern embarks on an ambitious task to construct a global deal (a framework for collaborative policy) on climate change and discusses on how that deal can be sustained against the backdrop of actual and potential catastrophic impacts of climate change to the existence of mankind today and to subsequent generations. Taking his point of departure from the 2006 Stern Review, Stern's chapter goes beyond it in a number of important ways in relation to subsequent policy discussions, new evidence and analysis, and discussions in the economics literature. Stern describes in detail an appropriate way to analyse the economics of climate change given the myriad of scientific and economic challenges posed, and suggests implications for emission targets, policy mechanisms and global actions. Stern contends that if one can bring the best economic analyses and judgements to the table as quickly as possible in real time, relevant and urgent policy decisions to counter climate change can be made rapidly and unambiguously. He adds that while the science of climate change is in abundance especially the argument that greenhouse gas (GHG) stocks and emissions are an externality, this must be complemented by economics which takes the science, particularly its analysis of risks, and thinks about its implications for policy — economic policy towards the risks of and from climate change.

In specific reference to economic policy analysis, Stern enumerates that the following must be placed at its core to centralise economics in the scientific understanding of climate change: (a) the economics of risk and uncertainty; (b) the links between economics and ethics as well as notions of responsibilities and rights in relation to others and the environment; and (c) role of international economic policy. Of central significance is the structure of argument on *stabilisation*: the choice of a stabilisation (stock) target shapes much of the rest of policy analysis because it carries significant implications for the permissible flow of emissions and therefore, for emissions reductions targets, which in turn shape the pricing and technology policies. By setting out the major risks from climate change, Stern suggests that these risks point to the need for both stock and flow targets, guided by an assessment of the costs involved in achieving them. In other words, Stern essentially argues that "the economics of risk points to the need for stock and flow quantity targets and the economics of costs and efficiency point to a price mechanism to achieve the targets".

Following this, the second section of Stern's chapter focuses on risks and how to reduce them, and on costs of abatement. Stern warns that while it is virtually impossible to be precise about the magnitude of the effects associated with temperature increases of 5°C for example, it does appear reasonable to assume that they would, more often than not, be catastrophic such as the melting of glaciers and sea-level rises, storms, floods and droughts, and loss of biodiversity. In a nutshell, Stern suggests, after looking back over a year, that subsequent evidence and analysis have confirmed the range of the cost estimates for stabilisation or indicated that they may be on the high side. He adds that effective policy combined with timely and judicious decision-making are crucial to keeping costs down. Stern also affirms that taking a clear view of a stabilisation goal allows for a measured and careful adjustment allowing for the replacement cycles of capital goods. He also cautions that if one adopted a 'wait-and-see' or 'climate policy ramp' approach, this risks not only excessive and dangerous levels of stocks but also much more costly abatement especially when there is subsequent realisation that the policy response was a delayed and inadequate one.

The third section of Stern's chapter examines policy and the role of different policy instruments. He opines that while a good policy instrument would be a price mechanism for GHGs which can serve as an incentive both to reduce GHG emissions and to keep costs of abatement down, it remains insufficient given the imperfections (North-South issues) in the world today. Four further planks of policy are deemed necessary, according to Stern. First is to embrace technology and accelerate its development. Second is to take account of information and transaction costs especially in relation to energy efficiency. Third is to provide an international framework to help with combating deforestation, which is subject to market failures. Fourth is to have a strong international focus so as to promote collaboration, take account of equity, and reduce global costs. In terms of pricing of externality of GHGs, Stern pointed out that this can be done in primarily three ways: (a) carbon taxation; (b) carbon training on the basis of trade in rights to emit which are allocated or auctioned; and (c) implicit pricing via regulations and standards which insist on constraints on actions or technologies which involve extra cost but imply reductions in emissions. Most-of-all, research and development in technologies also require sustained public support.

The last section of Stern's chapter details out the manifold components of a global deal on climate change. Stern argues that since climate change is global in its origins and in its impacts, an effective response must thus be organised globally and must involve international understanding and collaboration. Stern adds that this collaboration can only be established and sustained if it is underpinned by a shared appreciation that methods used are: (a) effective (on the scale required); (b) efficient (keep costs down); and (c) equitable (responsibilities and costs are allocated in ways which take account of wealth, ability and historical responsibility). On top of this, the solutions should be incentive-compatible, country-by-country political support must be built, and public support for action must be garnered and founded on the realisation that it is possible to construct collaborative policies that are effective, efficient and equitable. Stern also adds that it is imperative for an effective global deal to have the currently poor countries at its centre, and that it must involve an implicit or explicit understanding over the sharing of the "contents of the atmosphere".

Stern also lists out the key elements of a global deal: (a) targets and trade, and (b) funding. For the former (a), this includes confirming Heiligendamm 50 per cent cuts in world emissions by 2050 with rich country cuts at least 80 per cent; developing countries to take on targets at latest by 2020 and rich country reductions and trading schemes designed to be open to trade with other countries; and supply side from developing countries simplified to allow much bigger markets for emissions. For the latter (b), this includes strong initiatives, with public funding, on deforestation to prepare for inclusion in trading; demonstration and sharing of technologies; and rich countries to deliver on Monterrey and Gleneagles commitments on official development assistance (ODA) in the context of extra costs of development arising from climate change.

Stern reiterated in his conclusion that the challenge of climate change is a formidable one because it covers a large part of the economy, is long term, is filled with risk and uncertainty, is demanding internationally, is urgent due to the nature of the problem itself and the pace of public discussion and decision-making, and is a long-term problem for analysis. But Stern believes that a global deal on climate change presents the much-needed antidote to these challenges of climate change. It meets the criteria of effectiveness as it is on the right scale; efficiency as it relies heavily on markets and market-oriented innovation; and equitable as it does at least give some specificity to the "common but differentiated responsibility" already accepted internationally. Underpinning this is intensive public discussion and support which is the ultimate form of enforcement mechanism.

Despite having such a global deal with responsible policies, Stern warns that the world is likely to experience an additional 1–2°C of global warming over the 0.8°C it is going through today. Thus adaptation will be necessary worldwide though Stern concedes this would be particularly difficult for poor countries. That said, it would be perilous for policy-makers and in particular, economists to advocate weak policy and to procrastinate and delay under the pretext that more research needs to be done and it is better to "wait and see". Stern maintains that the time to act is now which would at least give mankind, at fairly modest cost, a cleaner world and environment even if it may seem, albeit improbable, that the vast majority of climate scientists have over-exaggerated or have got it simply wrong. A global deal is indeed an admirable starting point which calls for urgent and immediate action on climate change, and as Stern opines, will inspire further research as it requires collaboration across disciplines and at various levels of policy-making (national, regional, global). While not explicitly referring to Asia, one could infer from Stern's arguments that a global deal on climate change would be incomplete and fruitless without the inclusion of Asia and in particular, India and China which are one of the highest emitters of GHGs as well as Indonesia with the haze problem that continues to have a transnational impact on the other countries in Southeast Asia.

The chapters written in this book all converge to the point that despite challenges emanating from the politics of knowledge, Asia's renaissance and transformation will continue. Collectively, these chapters address the complex issues arising out of a knowledge-based economy especially after the 1997 AFC, redefinition of free speech and human rights, and deepening technological challenges facing Asia and the rest of the world in this epoch of rapid climate change. At the same time, these chapters specify solutions, and list out opportunities in tandem with these issues. It follows from these chapters that the outlook for Asia is a positive and an optimistic one. Knowledge science accompanied by ICT which appears to be widely available has revolutionised the relations between the West and the rest and in this case, Asia. Premier Lee similarly argues that with the complete and instant exposure to an overwhelming torrent of information through the Internet and other online channels, this brings great economic benefits and great potential for sharing and using knowledge as well as that it magnifies notable events across a global listening board.

In his work on the *Politics of Knowledge*, Edward Said introduced the concept of *worldliness* in which he talks about the "restoration of works and interpretations of their place in the global setting": this entails the "opposite of separatism" and the "reverse of exclusivism" in which the world embraces a "large many-windowed house of human culture as a whole".[6] By the same token, the chapters in this book espouse the concept of *worldliness* towards a quest and acquisition of knowledge that is anti-separatist and inclusive, which would ultimately benefit everyone regardless of the hemisphere one lives in. As the chapters will also demonstrate, similar to the arguments made by many other scholars such as Mahbubani, Asia wants to learn, replicate and collaborate, and not to overpower and dominate the West: Asia wants to be co-drivers and co-pilots of knowledge and technology. This is the Asian perspective.

Notes

1. Gerard Delanty, *Challenging Knowledge: The University in the Knowledge Society* (Philadelphia: The Society for Research into Higher Education and Open University Press, 2001) and Nico Stehr, *Knowledge Society* (London: Sage, 1994).
2. Mahbubani, Kishore, *The New Asian Hemisphere: The Irresistible Shift of Global Power to the East* (New York: Public Affairs, 2008).
3. Michel Foucault, *Power/Knowledge* (New York: Pantheon, 1977).
4. Edward W. Said, *Orientalism* (New York: Pantheon, 1978).

5. J. Boyle, "Enclosing the genome: What squabbles over genetic patents could teach us", *Perspectives on Properties of the Human Genome Project I* 50 (2003): 97–122.

6. Edward W. Said, *Reflections on Exile and Other Essays* (Cambridge, Massachusetts: Harvard University Press, 2000).

Chapter 3

TRUTH, FREE SPEECH AND KNOWLEDGE
The Human Rights Contribution
Conor Gearty

THE UNIVERSALITY OF HUMAN RIGHTS

Our understanding of knowledge underpins our attitude to free speech. If we agree that knowledge is composed of our grasping a set of truths that lie outside ourselves, then our main concern will be with how to access this understanding, how to unlock this truth. The role of the authority figure in the delivery of this knowledge is often critical in a culture that takes this approach to knowledge: it may be the priest or other kind of spiritual leader or it might be some Royal personage or other type of ruler with wide acceptability within the relevant community. In none of these situations is knowledge particularly problematic; nor is it generative of politics. In fact where truth is held by authority figures and passed on to a largely passive audience of subjects, 'free speech' will often be regarded as subversive rather than facilitative of truth: it will be seen as getting in the way of knowledge rather than as helping the discovery of it. This is why strong religious movements clamp down on speech (heresy) and authoritarian leaders lock people up for expressing their point of view (treason; 'terrorism').

The version of knowledge outlined above has not survived the rational scrutiny of the Enlightenment period. Starting with the reformation and moving through the revolutions of the 18th and 19th centuries into a 'post-modern' culture where knowledge is not characterised in absolute terms, we now see knowledge as something that is made not found, that we create out of our intercommunications rather than receive as tablets of stone from some higher authority. In such circumstances the politics of knowledge become key: whose version of truth is to be heard? Who can persuade whom? How do we reach agreement on what truth for now prevails? Here is where the importance of free speech becomes apparent: it is the vital oil in the machine of truth-manufacture that makes every modern society tick. In the 19th century, and borrowing from Darwin and Smith, Oliver Wendell Holmes developed this kind of pragmatic justification for free speech as creating a vital market-place in ideas. His insight remains as 'true' now as it was when he first developed it. Free speech is therefore vital to any successful, modern society which aims for self-government rather than subjugation.

This chapter discusses the unique contribution of human rights to the growth of a relative approach to knowledge which nevertheless requires for its effectiveness a commitment to one absolute, or near absolute, namely the principle of free speech. In section one the universality of human rights is restated and defended, in particular against relativist claims which argue that the very idea is itself a creature of colonial or imperial power. In part two, the universal meaning of human rights is further explored by consideration of the Asian values debate which has been such an important part of human rights discussions in the course of the past twenty years. The chapter ends with a brief concluding section summarising the argument for free speech as a vital guarantor of the freedom that only democratic forms of government can deliver and through which the flourishing of all — including the poor and the dispossessed — can be best secured. Properly understood neither human rights nor free speech is a hangover of colonialism; rather each is a vital ingredient in the successful effort that every society must make to face the future. There are of course limits and in this concluding part these will be located in the context of the underlying rationale of free speech.

One of the most damaging assertions about the idea of human rights is that it is inherently the possession of what we used to call the West and what might now be better described as the 'Global North'. On this analysis the subject is a Western construct, created at a particular moment in time to suit certain interests and now projected onto the world stage as an ethical mask behind which old imperial and colonial power continues to assert itself. The concrete realisations of human rights in law and practice are just ways of imposing a certain kind of humanity on a world that has no natural affinity with the shape that it is being required — in the name of human rights — to take. The ultimate expression of this perspective is to be found in the use of the language of human rights to underpin military conquest.[1] It is no wonder all self-respecting sovereign nations from outside this narrow club of old, industrialised states baulk at being manoeuvred in this way into such unfamiliar and uncomfortable territory.

This perspective is profoundly, utterly wrong, and it needs to be rejected. But in order to do so, we need first to recognise quite how strong the arguments are on which it relies and exactly how to refute them. The sceptics of universalism seem to have history, philosophy, international relations, politics and law on their side. In this part of this chapter I intend to show how this is the case but also why on a careful analysis it is more appearance than reality. My intention in doing so is to demonstrate that, far from being a challenge to local values, human rights understood in a certain way (which among other strengths prioritises free speech) represent a vindication of the best of those values. Viewed in this fashion, the idea of human rights is truly the universal ethical discourse for which its enthusiasts argue, albeit one that is particularly susceptible to being distorted to facilitate other, non-human-rights-based ends.

CULTURAL SPECIFICITY AND HUMAN RIGHTS

It is clear that the development of the idea of human rights has indeed been tied up with the story of the West. It starts with the Greeks (Plato; Aristotle; Epictetus), picks up some Roman pedigree on its way (Cicero) via the Catholic Church (from St Paul through Plotinus to Saint Thomas Aquinas) to northern Europe, where it settles down in England (Hobbes; Locke) and France (Rousseau), before setting up further outposts in the United States.[2] The hit list of early human rights documents is a hymn to the civilising progress of what we now think of as western statehood: Magna Carta in 1215, the American Declaration of Independence in 1776, the French Declaration of the Rights of Man and of the Citizen in 1789, and so on. Even the critique of human rights that was so powerful in the 19th century is an argument from within the intellectual culture: it is the work of Bentham, of Burke and of Marx[3] rather than of scholars and thinkers or even of activists drawn from outside the North altogether.

The philosophy of human rights is even more clearly narrowly focused. The development of the notion of objective right, the idea of a natural law determining right behaviour which stood above the people of the world and ordered their conduct, found expression through the intellectual work done in the dominant states and institutions of the early medieval period; the close connection between these writers and the centres of contemporary power has been such that their influence has continued to be felt. The power of the Roman Catholic Church may have been severely affected by schism and secularism but its hold on the Global North remains sufficiently strong for the writings of St Paul, St Augustine and St Thomas Aquinas to have entered into and to have remained embedded within that culture's mainstream.[4] The same is true of the great secularising work done by the 'Enlightenment' thinkers, among whom the most prominent for human rights purposes is Immanuel Kant (1724–1804). By developing a European identity at a critical juncture and then explaining the emergence of independent nations in a way that was satisfactory to the enquiring minds that underpinned power in such places, these thinkers found their prestige and authority indelibly linked to the fortunes of the then newly emerging European project of democratic politics at home and imperial aggrandisement abroad. The military and economic successes of these European colonial nations from the late 17th century right up until the end of the Second World War has meant that their intellectual apologists (using the latter term in a non-derogatory sense) have effortlessly found their place in the canon of great authors: when it comes to securing influence for one's ideas there is nothing as good as being associated with long-term political and military success.[5]

And it is quite clear that the idea of human rights (including pre-eminently free speech) was central to the democratising and hence to the ethical foundations of many of these new national powers. The long drawn-out English revolution of 1642–89 which prepared the way for British power was ultimately resolved by a conscious reliance on the supposed natural right of Englishmen to do away with a regal power that was not to their fancy: in this way could economic self-interest be camouflaged by an apparently universalist ethic.[6] In 1789, the French Declaration of the Rights of Man and of the Citizen was even clearer on how it was the demand for human rights that propelled its people into revolt. As the opening words of that stirring document put it, 'The representatives of the French people, organised in National Assembly, considering that ignorance, forgetfulness, or contempt of the rights of man are the sole causes of public misfortunes and of the corruption of governments, have resolved to set forth in a solemn declaration the natural, inalienable, and sacred rights of man.' The European nations that turned their attention to global domination in the 19th century were not merely selfish entities in search of prosperity at the expense of others: they saw themselves as ethical movements, forces for good in the world, civilisers with the right (and only) God and the right (and only) philosophical foundation in (their version of) human rights.

There are many who would acknowledge the Western origins of human rights as set out above but who would then go on to say that the subject has made a fresh start in recent decades. They would point in particular to the resurgence of human rights, and of international human rights law in particular, which has been such a dramatic part of the international scene since the end of the Second World War. It is certainly the case that the (European) idea of national sovereignty has been modified to some (but only some) extent by the emphasis on individual rights (including free speech) that is now to be found in documents like the Universal Declaration of Human Rights (1948) and the International Covenants on Civil and Political Rights and on Economic, Social and Cultural Rights that were agreed at the

United Nations in 1966. But the very prominence of human rights over the past sixty years has stemmed from its value to the great powers, and in particular American power.[7] It is not a disgrace to our subject to recognise that it offered an appealing alternative to (and protection from) socialism to those with responsibility for establishing a new world order in the aftermath of the defeat of the Axis powers in 1945.[8] On this view the individual rights set out both in the Universal Declaration and in such regional instruments as the European Convention on Human Rights and Fundamental Freedoms (1950) have served to institutionalise a way of looking at the world that is — in Marxist terms — unacceptably monadist[9] and restrictive of state power: on this analysis free speech in the hands of individuals is merely a power to make mischief, to disrupt efforts at progressive reform, its roots remaining indelibly Western — and capitalist.

THE VIRTUE OF HUMAN RIGHTS AS A FLOATING SIGNIFIER[10]

As indicated in the introductory remarks to this chapter, the sceptical direction that thought has taken in the West has shaken the confidence in truth upon which the idea of human rights has previously depended. This has implications for the universality debate: if human rights are no longer 'true' for the North, how can they be true for the world at large? How can the critical, perhaps even cynical, analysis with which the last section ended be avoided? The way the subject has responded to this challenge to its integrity has opened a route to a new set of foundations which are less rooted in the work of European thinkers of the past and consequently better able to connect across continents and cultures than this past, highly localised narrative has been able to do. The delocalisation of the idea has involved the peeling away of a number of culturally-specific layers now widely regarded as largely extraneous. The subject has shed its narrowly philosophical layer which has assumed that it can be understood only by those familiar with a particular European narrative centred on but not limited to the writings of Immanuel Kant. It has also escaped the lawyers' assumption that it is a wholly legal subject with a content made up entirely of the rights that form the basis of international human rights law, whatever they might be at any particular moment in time. Third, the idea of human rights has embraced the radical uncertainty that has been such a prominent feature of (post) modern thought, and which is potentially so subversive of its essence, by reconfiguring its core attributes not as rights as such but rather in terms of the values that underpin those rights.[11]

Perhaps surprisingly, it has not proved difficult to identify what the human values are that lie behind the idea of human rights, giving it the intellectual fuel that was previously supplied by faith and reason.[12] They include respect for human dignity, for the liberty and autonomy of the individual and for the principle of representative government according to law. Free speech principles are suffused through all of these. There is a new emphasis on the virtue of tolerance and a commitment to respect for diversity: in this way has the idea of human rights cleverly co-opted the collapse of certainty that in its different and earlier shapes threatened its very existence. At bottom, the subject flows out of two basic propositions, that human kind should not be treated in a cruel way (the negative fundamental) and that each and every person should be given the chance to flourish as a human being, to do the best they can with the capabilities they have (the positive fundamental). As to the foundations of such fundamentals, the beauty of the human rights discourse — and its durability — lies in the way in which different audiences can find their own roots for these various insights: the respect for diversity that is now one of the core values at the heart of human rights applies also to the supply of reasons for their importance. Some have been comfortable with continuing with the notion of human rights as rooted in a series of religious insights about man and woman's relationship with his or her creator. Others have felt no need to junk centuries of Enlightenment philosophy just to stay in touch with post-modern fashions. Those persuaded by such critiques have nevertheless felt able to believe in the values underpinning human rights as basic facts of evolutionary life. Radical human rights critics root the truth of their advocacy of the subject in the way that it supplies an empowering language for the vulnerable and the powerless, and this is enough for them. It is not a slight to say that human rights 'means all things to all men (and women)'; rather it is the key that explains their survival and continued extraordinary success. But on any of these meanings, intersecting across their different circles of content, free speech is key.

ASIAN VALUES AND HUMAN RIGHTS

So how does all this play outside the Global North? In the first half of the 1990s, the relationship between human rights and what were described as Asian values came briefly to the fore as a topic of the first importance, one that for a time seemed to threaten the universality of human rights, forcing its ethical assumptions onto the defensive and (at its most extreme) suggesting that respect for human rights (and free speech) was little more than a provincial piece of Western thinking for which the rest of the world should have no sensible use. Forged in the exciting crucible of a set of countries whose economic prosperity was such that their leaders had convinced themselves that they had found the capitalistic Midas touch, 'Asian values' were to decline just as the inexorability of these nations' prosperity ground to a halt: in retrospect we can see that it was an idea too closely linked to a passing sense of superiority of the leaders of a few small states, too reliant on economic (rather than intellectual) power. The challenge it posed to human rights did however appear for a while to be a fundamental one, and the response developed to it has helped frame the subject's recent history, and to reinforce the developments that have been identified at the end of the last section. The human rights idea has emerged stronger from its joust with 'Asian values', better able to stand up for itself, to frame the right responses to cultural critiques, and in the process has jettisoned baggage from the past that does not fit with what the idea of human rights entails today. Our subject owes a great deal to the 'Asian values' critique: it has made it a fitter and leaner intellectual, political and activist beast.

The Bangkok Declaration[13]

The main stimulation for the emergence of the Asian values perspective was the World Conference on Human Rights, held in Vienna in 1993. This was a major event so far as women's human rights were concerned, the high point of a campaign which had been heavily critical of human rights discourse from a feminist perspective. The protagonists of this discourse sought to develop a new way of looking at human rights, and in particular were keen to break down the idea that human rights was only about the public sphere (the state and the individual) and not the private realm as well. The issue was important to feminists because of increased appreciation of the fact that there was great abuse of power (and therefore it was said breaches of human rights) within the realm of personal relations, and in particular within the husband/wife and family spaces. Thus on this account, violence within the home involved serious human rights violation that had hitherto been neglected. This opening up of human rights to a discourse based on power may seem straightforward today but it was highly innovative at the time — and very challenging. Vienna was to be about women's rights, but it was also — inevitably as a major human rights forum — to be about civil and political rights, including the usual civil liberties (expression, assembly, association and so on) which were a core part of the human rights story, entirely orthodox in comparison to women's rights, but none the less difficult for national leaders whose sympathy with expressions of dissent was — to put it mildly — very limited. These two sets of agendas were disturbing to a number of leaders of Asian countries, including in particular the then senior minister of Singapore Lee Kuan Yew and Malaysia's prime minister Dr Mahathir bin Mohamad. The Chinese leadership was also predictably uncertain about the human rights agenda.

In preparation for Vienna, the Asian States adopted a statement, the Bangkok Declaration, containing 'the aspirations and commitments of the Asian region' with regard to human rights. Its opening recitals made various non-controversial statements of loyalty to human rights, but there were a sufficient number of a different sort among them to suggest something other than mild obeisance before a universal force. There were three themes underlying these statements which set the Asian leadership that agreed them apart from the conventional human rights thinking of the day. First there is the matter of fair application: the approach to human rights had to be 'balanced'; 'double standards in the implementation of human rights' were to be avoided; 'concern' was expressed about the priority accorded 'one category of rights' (including free speech); 'economic, social, cultural, civil and political rights' were interdependent and indivisible and had therefore to be 'addressed in an integrated and balance manner'. The barely disguised subtext here was that civil and political rights (with their assertions of democratic and protest rights) had been wrongly prioritised by the supporters of human rights in the Global North. In fact from the Bangkok perspective, social and economic rights were of *at least* equal importance. Second the declaration introduced the notion of regional values as potentially in opposition to human rights. The 'diverse and rich cultures and traditions' of Asia needed to be better recognised. '[C]confrontation and the imposition of incompatible values' were to be avoided. Though 'universal in nature', human rights must, as the substance of the declaration went on to say, 'be considered in the context of a dynamic and evolving process of international norm-setting, bearing in mind the significance of national and regional particularities and various historical, cultural and religious backgrounds'.

Third there was the importance of the right to development, not only of particular countries but in relation as well to the development of 'a just and fair world economic order'. The right was 'an integral part of fundamental human rights, which must be realized through international cooperation, respect for fundamental human rights, the establishment of a monitoring mechanism and the creation of essential international conditions for the realization of such right'. It is economic and social progress (rather than one supposes this or that international oversight body) that 'facilitates the growing trend towards democracy and the promotion and protection of human rights'. The forthcoming world conference should take a 'just' approach to human rights. So the Declaration itself goes on to '[d]iscourage any attempt to use human rights as a conditionality for extending development assistance'. It calls for the 'non-use of human rights as an instrument of political pressure' and reiterates 'that all countries, large and small, have the right to determine their political systems, control and freely utilize their resources, and freely pursue their economic, social and cultural development'.

The Bangkok Declaration had an impact out of proportion to the relative restraint of the language that it used. The Vienna Declaration adopted by the world conference on human rights on 25 June 1993[14] did not however shy away from restating some human rights absolutes:

> All human rights are universal, indivisible and interdependent and interrelated. The international community must treat human rights globally in a fair and equal manner, on the same footing, and with the same emphasis. While the significance of national and regional particularities and various historical, cultural and religious backgrounds must be borne in mind, it is the duty of States, regardless of their political, economic and cultural systems, to promote and protect all human rights and fundamental freedoms.

The 1993 Conference witnessed the high-water mark of the Asian values controversy. Severe economic downturns in the late 1990s distracted the states from which the most biting critique of human rights had emerged. Ratification of the international human rights conventions has continued across the Asia-Pacific region, not as quickly as human rights advocates might like certainly, but the graph of engagement has been pushing upwards rather than downwards. The strong leaders associated with the Bangkok Declaration have left office, being replaced in peaceful processes that have tended both to ignite and then to deepen calls for democratic renewal from within the countries concerned: such reforming energy from within civil society inevitably undercuts claims that human rights and democracy are alien forces to be resisted rather than embraced. The machinery of human rights monitoring, led by the UN and aided and abetted by the ever-vigilant NGO community, continues to track human rights abuses in the Asian-Pacific region without any undue embarrassment rooted in supposedly illegitimate interferences in culture or tradition.[15] It would be tempting to conclude that the passing squall of 1993 can now be safely forgotten, a passing blip on the stately progress of universal human rights. But this would be to take exactly the wrong approach: the critique offered in 1993 is of the first importance to our subject, and the answers developed by way of response have shaped the form that contemporary human rights have taken.

CONFRONTING THE ASIAN VALUES CRITIQUE

Much of what was said both in the Bangkok Declaration itself but more especially in the course of the discussions and debates that surrounded it hit home precisely because of the underlying legitimacy of many of the basic points that fuelled the antagonism of the sceptics. As we saw in part one of this chapter, human rights as a subject has emerged out of the European intellectual tradition and in recent years it has taken a shape that has been largely the creation of the governments and NGO activists of the big economic powers in the northern hemisphere. Focusing very much on this narrative, the Declaration made some telling points about a *version* of human rights and thought that as a result it had dealt the whole subject a deadly body blow. In fact it had grazed only a part of the body, leaving the vital organs untouched. For the features of human rights that are fundamental to the medium to long term well-being of the subject go much deeper than the use to which the term has been put by this or that state power, and in doing so reach towards a set of universal statements about the human condition that transcend the local.

The meaning of the term 'human rights' has changed over time but in its essentials it stands for a perspective on human conduct that is the exclusive preserve of no single culture or peoples.[16] This is the point of view that asserts that it is wrong to engage in cruel or inhuman or degrading treatment towards another person, that humiliation along these lines is to be prohibited whoever the victim might be, in other words whether he or she is friend or foe, neighbour or stranger is neither here nor there. This attitude flows out of a commitment to respect the humanity of the other, to see in the person outside of oneself an image of oneself, and not to depersonalise the other by replacing this species-solidarity with other images (rooted in nationality, or ethnicity, or beliefs for example) that emphasise difference. If this prohibition on cruelty and humiliation represents an important part of what is meant by human rights, so too does a second line of conduct captured by the phrase — the behaving well towards the other in the sense of facilitating the opportunity to lead a full life, to grow as a person and to do the best that can be achieved with the talents that are to hand. This is the bit of the human rights story that not only forbears from hostility but positively welcomes as well, that not only does not slam the door in the stranger's face but gives him or her a chance to carve out a decent niche in the accommodation within.

The foundations of this stance towards humanity matter less for the present than the fact of its pervasiveness: there are few cultures in the world that have not got some consistent strain within them that preaches this kind of species solidarity, this openness to the stranger, this willingness to give everyone a chance to flourish.[17] Now clearly this is not the same as saying that a human-rights-abiding culture is inherently pacifist — these tropes of hospitality do not require a family, tribe or peoples irrationally to drop its guard or to overcome its (stronger?) tendencies both towards ensuring the survival of its own people and in the direction of mixing only with those it knows, its own kind within a human family made up of many strange members. In its universalist shape, human rights stands for the capacity for outreach and for empathy with the stranger that is in evolutionary terms at least as important to the success of the species as the more short or medium term emphasis on the survival in isolation from others of this or that community, ethnic group or nation. Just as a family relishes its autonomy and collective solidarity while knowing at the same time that to survive and to grow it has to welcome strangers into its very core, so too have gatherings of peoples since the start of time known that to reach out and intermingle with strangers is to grow stronger as a people, different perhaps but all the better for the intermingling that openness to the stranger has allowed. Human rights is one of the terms that we use today to describe this posture of empathy, this curiosity towards the stranger, that has been such an important thread in human development. There are others of course; often these are religious in form, relying upon divine assertions or some other kind of spiritual guidance from outside or even deeply within the self. Human rights has no objection to the deployment of other language to capture its account of humanity, indeed has drawn strength in the past from exactly such foundations, but in today's mode it does not *depend* on any such interventions, celestial or otherwise.

To identify this as the core of the human rights message is not to deny the subject its place in cut and thrust of history. Of course the term has been abused in the past, and continues to be distorted today.[18] It does not follow from this concession, however, that one must argue for a jettisoning of the entire human rights vocabulary. The politicisation of the past (the use made of the work of Locke and Rousseau by English and French revolutionaries for example) has helped with the overall human rights project, by reducing opportunities for cruelty (through creating a momentum for democracy) and by theorising a perspective on the person that has highlighted the individual's entitlement to pursue his or her own life plans, thereby bolstering the important human rights idea of personal freedom. And even where the term is manifestly being abused, used to underpin colonial aggression for example or the abuse of strangers as necessary to a civilisation's survival, the essential meaning of the phrase can be deployed to expose as a lie this attempt to make the term the servant of the particular. If human rights as a subject cannot claim this universal core then it has no basis to fight off those who would plunder its substance for selfish gain.

When we analyse the Asian values critique from this perspective, we can see that it misses many central points.[19] At an abstract level, it is manifestly clear that the values of hospitality, active compassion and respect for the person that underpin this idea of universal human rights are not absent from Asian culture; rather they are a vital element in that culture, the thread in the narrative that makes these places and peoples warm and open to the stranger, that emphasises solidarity with (rather than hostility towards) the other. The notion of representative government too is not alien — many communities have enjoyed this kind of autonomy in the Asian region in the past and increasingly many are managing to secure it in the present as well. It would surely be condescending, even fatuous, to say to a South Korean, a Taiwanese or (these days) a Singaporean that their determination to secure a collective say over their destinies is merely to display their commitment to foreign values. And while the *format* of judicial review of the exercise of governmental power may be a result of relatively recent interactions with imperial and colonial power, the *substance* of what is being secured — government according to pre-ordained rules — is hardly a western invention.

In truth, as with all nations, cultures and peoples, there are different stories supporting not one but various understanding of themselves and while some of these are 'human rights' accounts, others are not — and the two can sometimes be in a tense relationship with each other. So the thread of patriarchy that is undeniably to be found in Asian society is not easily reconciled with a commitment to human rights that values individual freedom in a gender-free way. Nor is the paternalistic version of Asian society that emphasises leadership and downgrades individual choice easy to fit within democratic models of decision-making with its commitment to the equal involvement of all. The point to draw from this is not that the human rights perspective is therefore inauthentic or in some way invalid; it is rather that there are different threads to a culture and these are not always consistent. It is of course exactly the same with any Global North country that one cares to mention: the human rights abiding nation that kills prisoners after shambolic trials; the constitutional democracy that locks up foreign suspected terrorists without trial; the freedom-loving state that uses military power to kill hundreds of thousands of foreigners to secure its interests on the world stage; and so on.

Double standards are not the result of some malfunction in the rationality of government; rather they are what occur when different parts of a country's story produce conflicting outcomes at the same time. This takes us to the final observation on 'Asian values' — the question of who benefits from their being adopted in a way that crowds out all the other threads in a culture's history and tradition. The answer is invariably that it is the powerful who stand to gain from reliance on alleged indigenous traditions to see off external criticism: the state leadership that is disinclined to subject its power to internal scrutiny; the family head that enjoys the control that a particular reading of the culture gives him over his family members; the business executive who sees in such 'tradition' an attractive way in which to hold organised labour at bay; the industrialist whose version of his country's past allows him to say that basic health and safety standards need not apply in his factories. Human rights standards are not an alien intrusion in such circumstances. They are the vital means by which countries subject to such practices can reassert the better parts of their culture's history and thereby recover and secure their own version of the universal good.

CONCLUSION

The universality of the kind of human rights message set out at the end of the last section has particular and immediate implications for truth, free speech and knowledge. A human rights commitment of the type delineated there is not one in which any particular culture or code of laws has superiority. Rather its project is a universalist one, committed to the avoidance of cruelty on the one hand and to personal growth on the other. The first of these entails as close a commitment to truth as our subject is ever likely to come, namely that the torturing of another, or the treating or punishing of them in a way that is inhuman and/or degrading is to dehumanise them to such a point that a basic universal taboo has been breached. The second involves a strong adherence to the kind of open society that free speech makes possible, a place where within the limits of a modestly defined law the people can do their own thing, grow in their own way as individuals or as part of a group or association. Democracy necessitates this kind of commitment to free speech, just as it must determinedly protect political freedom so as to avoid the channels of change in its representative system being choked off by power, privilege or by vested interests.

It will be immediately apparent from these remarks that while the Asian critique discussed here may have originated in a discussion that took place in the 1990s, it remains depressingly relevant today. The farcical journey of the Olympic torch across the world en route to Beijing for the 2008 Olympic Games became a symbol not of harmony but of different perspectives on human rights. On the one hand there were those who felt strongly that attention should be drawn wherever possible to the human rights situation in general in China and to the Tibetan question in particular. On the other side were the Chinese leadership and its friends, furious at the disorder that accompanied what should have been a celebration of harmony. The Chinese people themselves appeared to share the view of the Communist Party that runs their country, but in a highly controlled society of the sort that China is it is impossible to be sure of what the people (as a collective entity) think or to be sure even if we did know this that the attitude they have adopted is an informed one. It was clear throughout Spring 2008 that resentment at the treatment of the torch in Global North countries was fuelled by a scepticism about human rights that in turn represented something of a reworking of the Asian values discussions of the past.

The critique is not all one way however. It would be wrong to assume that just because a place calls itself democratic that it has the right level of commitment to free speech guaranteed within its state laws and practices. The leadership of many of the new democracies of the post Cold War era have been regularly tempted to clamp down on political speech, to force political opponents out of business, to control the media and so on, all the while maintaining that the fact of a periodic election establishes, without more, their democratic credentials. The true democrat, committed not only to elections but also to the open discussion that makes holding them worthwhile, rejects such a narrow view of what the subject is about. The established democracies may have settled upon the forms of free speech but these too are vulnerable to criticism on the basis of the extent to which power and money can influence public debate to far too great an extent than a proper open discussion would allow. So the commitment to free speech as a source of political knowledge involves a strong critique not only of non-democratic or partly-democratic states but also of well-entrenched democratic nations as well. The human rights perspective rooted in a set of fundamental principles, demonstrates once again the impartiality of its universalist, critical eye.

Proponents of human rights acknowledge however that free speech cannot be untrammelled. No one is allowed falsely to call fire in a crowded cinema, just as the guarantee cannot be used to allow an inciter of murder to escape unpunished. Principle guides not only the range of our rights but also when they can be properly qualified. Is this expression necessary to our well-being in the sense of being required to facilitate our flourishing as a person in our own way? Does this engagement in speech have a political dimension so that it should be viewed as a contribution to our evolving sense of truth in the public sphere? Is the person speaking an elected representative or a candidate for election? Or to look at the point from the other angle, is what is being said without any worth even viewed from the perspective of the speaker or listener? Is it valueless trivia or tittle-tattle? Is it defamatory or obscene or motivated by hate? Democratic states control speech in different ways, with much depending on the background culture and history of the place in question: holocaust denial is a more sensitive issue in Germany than in the United States, for example. The important point is not which restrictions are embraced but rather how they are arrived at and how broad they are in their application. As long as the process of restriction is democratic and respect for free speech principles is built into the operation of such laws, the defender of human rights is not likely to be indelibly opposed to them as a matter of principle. The proponent of human rights is no extremist arguing in a vacuum within which politics does not operate. It is this awareness of limitations that gives added cogency to the argument for universality set out above.

Notes

1. See M. Ignatieff, *The Lesser Evil. Political Ethics in an Age of Terror* (Edinburgh: Edinburgh University Press, 2004).
2. J. Mahoney, *The Challenge of Human Rights* (Basil Blackwell Publishing, Oxford, 2007); M. R. Ishay, *The Human Rights Reader*, 2nd ed. (London: Routledge, 2007).
3. J. Waldron, ed., 'Nonsense upon Stilts': Bentham, Burke and Marx on the *Rights of Man* (London: Methuen, 1987).
4. For continuing influence see M. J. Perry, *Towards a Theory of Human Rights. Religion, Law, Courts* (New York: Cambridge University Press, 2007), ch 2.
5. Douzinas, *Human Rights and Empire: The Political Philosophy of Cosmopolitanism* (Abingdon: Routledge-Cavendish, 2007).
6. A. C. Grayling, *Towards the Light. The Story of the Struggles for Liberty & Rights That Made the Modern West* (London: Bloomsbury, 2007).
7. N. Guilhot, *The Democracy Makers. Human Rights and the Politics of Global Order* (New York: Columbia University Press, 2005); L. Hunt, *Inventing Human Rights: A History* (New York: W W Norton, 2007).
8. M. Mandel, "A Brief History of the New Constitutionalism, or 'How We Changed Everything so that Everything Remained the Same' ", 32 *Israel Law Review* 250, 1998.
9. On which see further Waldron, note 3 above.
10. See C. Douzinas, *The End of Human Rights* (Oxford: Hart Publishing, 2000).
11. Emancipation from the rigours of law is necessary but dangerous:

necessary because law is narrow; dangerous because values can be seized upon by the powerful and distorted. The battle over which values underpin human rights can determine whether one if for or against coercive interrogation, invasion, internment and so on from a human rights point of view — see Ignatieff, note 1 above, criticised by C. A. Gearty, 'With a Little Help From Our Friends', 34 *Index on Censorship* 36, 2005.

12. For a more detailed development of the argument set out in this paragraph, see Gearty, note 16 below, ch 2.

13. See generally M. Jacobsen and O. Brun, eds., *Human Rights and Asian Values. Contesting National Identities and Cultural Representations in Asia* (Surrey: Curzon Press, Richmond, 2000).

14. The final declaration at Vienna is in M. R. Ishay, *The Human Rights Reader* (London: Routledge, 1997), pp 479–91.

15. E.g. Human Rights Watch, World Report 2006 (New York 2006), especially Part 3 on Asia.

16. I develop these points further in *Can Human Rights Survive?* (Cambridge: Cambridge University Press, 2006).

17. This explains the ease with which practically every country in the world embraced the Universal Declaration of Human Rights: leaving aside enforcement it was possible for everyone to believe in the rights (whatever about rendering them real in specific situations: a different task altogether).

18. C. Douzinas, *Human Rights and Empire. The Political Philosophy of Cosmopolitanism* (London: Routledge-Cavendish, 2007).

19. And for a strong critique developing fresh points as well as those covered here see J. Donnelly, *Universal Human Rights in Theory and Practice*, 2nd ed. (Ithaca and London: Cornell University Press, 2003), ch 7.

Chapter 4

KNOWLEDGE
The Driver of Economic Growth
Danny Quah

INTRODUCTION

A calamitous financial crisis recently caused economies and
markets to collapse. Easy credit and a lack of financial system
transparency had led to excessive borrowing at low interest
rates. This last had fuelled a boom in housing, property, and
asset markets across tightly-coupled economies. The economy
at the centre of this maelstrom had its current account deficit
balloon to a record 8 per cent of GDP. Investors realised all this
was unsustainable and took corrective action. A catastrophic
crisis ensued: asset values plunged by up to 70 per cent; real
incomes plummeted in different countries by 11 per cent to as
much as 35 per cent; millions of people lost their jobs.

What I have just related, however, is not the 2007 U.S.
subprime mortgage-sparked credit crunch, although the latter
still might emerge to be that. The 8 per cent-current account
deficit country is not the U.S., but instead Thailand. The date on
those events was 1997–98, not 2007–08. The 'tightly-coupled

economies' were not the U.S. and Western Europe but instead the collection of Thailand, the East Asian Tiger economies, and the rest of emerging Asia. Those were the economies that, a decade ago, were viewed to be the catastrophes of corporate and political misgovernance, financial excess and wasteful over-investment. Yet, before 1997, those same countries had been held up as the growth miracles and poster children of a then-emerging consensus on managed economic development.

The year 1997 was a watershed. Ideas about successful economic development changed. Confidence in and on East Asia was shaken. Countries such as Singapore experienced for the first time in the modern era unemployment and stagnation. The names of Paul Krugman and my LSE colleague Alwyn Young grew identified with the idea that East Asia had come so far, so quickly through "mere sweat" — i.e., nothing miraculous in productivity but simply hard work and high savings — a growth strategy that ultimately must be unsustainable. A decade after those tumultuous events, once again emerging Asia has surprised. The post-1997 Asian reality has turned out to be a success, mostly, and very different from expectation a decade ago. Perhaps important lessons were learnt very quickly, and key repairs immediately put in place. Perhaps, for instance, the Economic Review Committee formed in December 2001 in Singapore under the Ministry of Trade and Industry had successfully done its job. Or perhaps 1997 was really just a blip, and fundamentals in emerging Asia have always been strong.

I do not think enough evidence has accumulated yet for us to be confident on the underlying causes. But we should try to be clear at least on the facts. In my view, two facts are central: first, the strength of emerging Asia has shifted eastwards the global balance of economic activity. Second, that shifting balance has profoundly lifted human welfare worldwide, more than perhaps anything else has done in the last 100 years.

The world economy after 1997 has underperformed by about 10 per cent relative to trend. A log-linear trend fitted to world GDP 1975–97 over-predicts the out-turn every year between 1998 and 2005 except for the single year 2000. The accumulated over-prediction amounts to US$3.3 trillion, or 9.7 per cent of trend.

FACTS

If there has been economic underperformance since 1997, the entire world has shown it (Figure 4.1). Global GDP has in the last decade come in at an accumulated shortfall of 10 per cent relative

FIGURE 4.1
Market Exchange Rates, 1975–2005

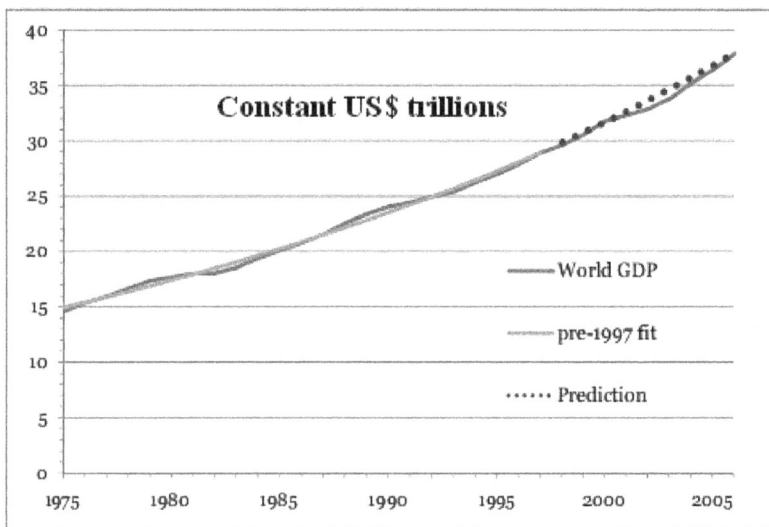

to the best (smoothed) guess based on information up through 1997.

What Emerging Asia has done in the global economy is hold things together and keep world economic growth going. Figure 4.2 shows what happened before and after 1997, the G7 (excluding Japan) on the left; Emerging Asia on the right.[1] The share of world GDP at market exchange rates is in light grey; the share of world growth is in dark grey. I have excluded Japan from the G7 bloc but the point I want to make would simply be strengthened if I put it back in.

Figure 4.2 shows that the G7 share of world GDP remains high. However, both before and after 1997, growth across the G7 has come in lower than shares there. This means two things: first, G7 growth has been lower than growth in the rest of the world; and second, the G7 share of world GDP is shrinking through time. By contrast, Emerging Asia has its growth much larger than

FIGURE 4.2
Emerging Asia Held Things Together

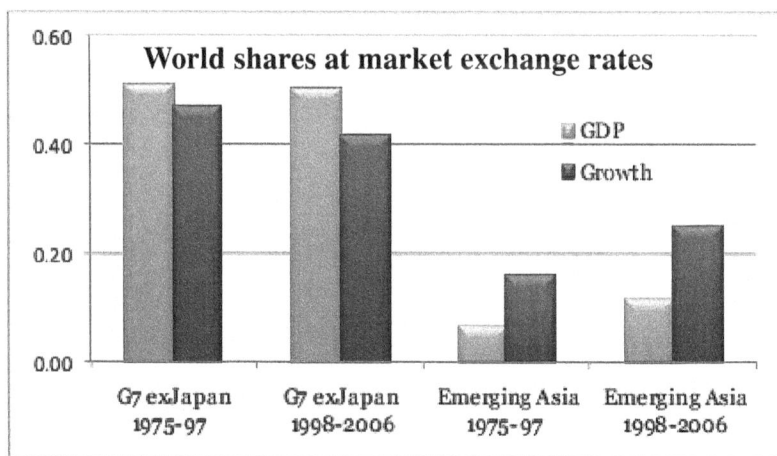

its share, both before and after 1997. If anything, growth has simply gotten even stronger and accelerated after 1997.

Crisis or otherwise, Emerging Asia continues to pull east the world's centre of gravity. In Crisis Tigers, I include those economies that had suffered the most from the 1997 currency crisis and those previously called the East Asian Tigers, i.e., Hong Kong, Taiwan, Singapore, and South Korea. See also Figure 4.4.

It is as if 1997 was just an irrelevance. This strengthened growth has occurred throughout Emerging Asia, whether one looks at those economies that had suffered the worst ravages of the Asian financial crisis, those East Asian Tigers thought to have over-saved and over-invested, or the billion-people economies China and India. Except for Indonesia, Taiwan, and Thailand, every economy in Emerging Asia has contributed to world growth more after 1997 than before (Figure 4.4). The bars indicate percentage share of world economic growth.

FIGURE 4.3
World Shares at Market Exchange Rates

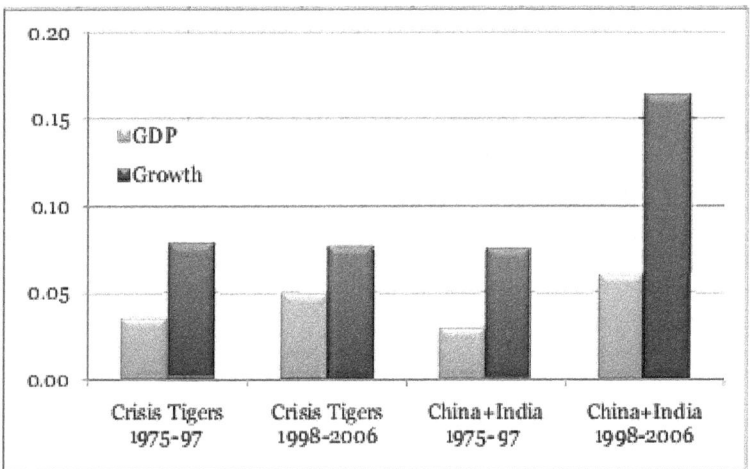

FIGURE 4.4
Contributors to World Growth, 1975–2006

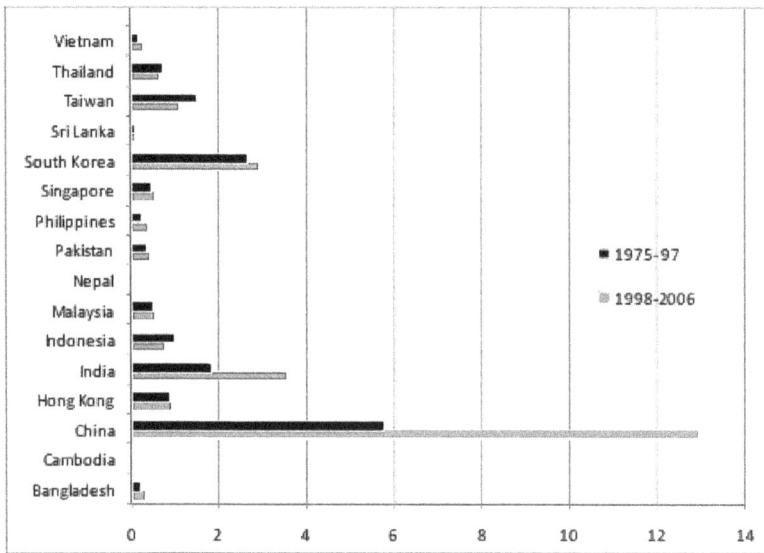

Crisis or not, Emerging Asia pulls east the world's centre of gravity.

Even at market exchange rates, rather than only at PPP, China and India together already contribute as much as does the U.S. to world economic growth (Table 4.1).

ASIDE: LSE AND EMERGING ASIA

Sometimes, when I am sitting in my office at LSE and mulling over these numbers, I think I see the answer. Literally, I do not mean I see the answer in some mathematical formula in my mind, I mean I see the answer literally. Figures 4.5 and 4.6 show

TABLE 4.1
Fraction of World Gross National Income and Absolute Growth, 2005–06 (at market exchange rates)

	2005 Fraction of World GNI	*2006 Growth, billions US$*
U.S.	28.6%	553.1
China	5.0%	371.8
India	1.8%	102.5
China + India	6.8%	474.3

FIGURE 4.5
LSE Student Composition, 2004–07

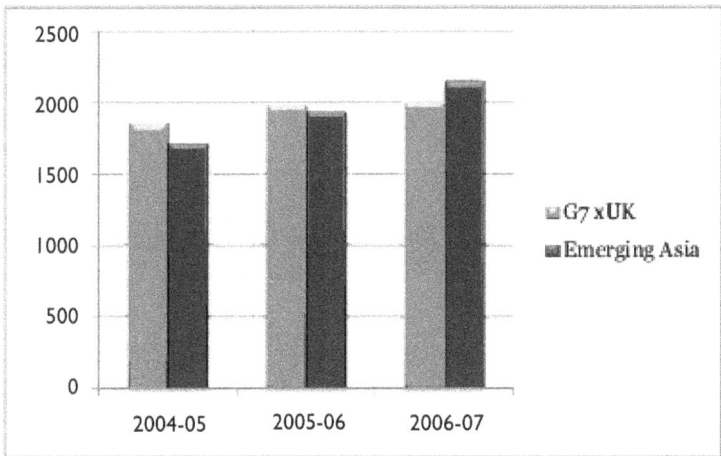

the composition of the LSE student population, broken down across the G7 (excluding the U.K.) and Emerging Asia. These two blocs have for a while now provided about an equal number of LSE students, with the G7 typically slightly more. In 2006/07, however, emerging Asia forged ahead, providing 2,153 students at the LSE compared to the G7's 2,001.

FIGURE 4.6
LSE Foreign Student Composition, 2004–07

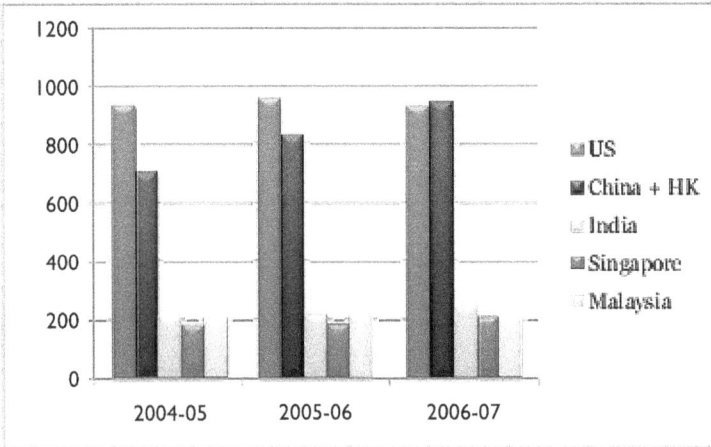

China until recently provided the LSE fewer students than the U.S.; in 2006/07 that configuration switched. India is snapping at the heels of China's lead and will seek to catch up. Well, perhaps LSE's changing student body simply reflects the changing balance of world income, rather than guides it. But there is always the possibility that the students we have trained at LSE do go out and, as we tell them to do, change the world. Do good in the world by doing well for oneself (and, of course, LSE's investment bankers, generally, do very well for themselves).

WORLD POVERTY

Whichever the right view might be, economic strength in Emerging Asia both before and after 1997 has not just shifted eastwards the global centre of gravity and significantly supported world economic growth. It has done more. Over the last quarter century Emerging Asia has lifted out of extreme poverty hundreds of millions of people. Indeed in that time China alone has done that for half a billion of its citizens. Five hundred million turns out also to be exactly the same number of people lifted out of poverty across the entire world in this time (Table 4.2).

TABLE 4.2
Poverty, 1981–2004

	1981	*1990*	*1999*	*2004*
World GDP 10^{12} PPP$	24	33	43	52
GDP per capita PPP$	5,408	6,292	7,231	8,198
World's poor 10^6	1,470	1,247	1,109	969
China's poor 10^6	634	374	223	128
Remainder 10^6	836	873	886	841

Note: Poor denotes people living on less than 1 Intl2000$ a day. These numbers are calculated from Chen and Ravallion (2007) and World Bank (2007).

Outside China, the number of the world's poor has remained flat, reflecting the interplay among economic growth in general, changing inequalities, and a rising population. However, the result, put mischievously and inaccurately but vividly, is that everyone lifted out of poverty in the world in the last quarter century … has been Chinese.

Obviously not every Asian country confronted with the same external global economy has taken the same growth path. The difference between China and India is striking (Figure 4.3).

China and India have differed dramatically in their alleviation of poverty. The horizontal axis shows per capita GDP in PPP; the vertical axis, millions of people living on less than $1 a day. These numbers are calculated from Chen and Ravallion (2007)

FIGURE 4.7
Growth and $1 – Day Poverty

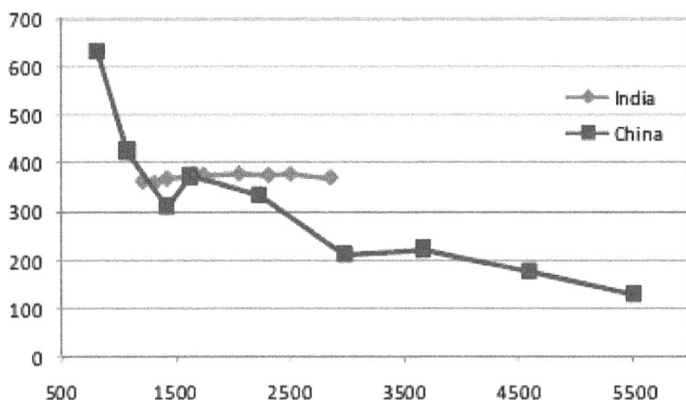

and World Bank (2007). They are shown for 3-yearly intervals from 1981 through 2002, and then 2004.

While in China the number of people living on less than $1 a day fell from 634 million in 1981 to 128 million in 2004, that same figure in India has barely budged, actually rising from 364 million to 371 million in this time. Overall growth in China raised per capita GDP from $804 to $5,493 (measured at PPP) but that in India only from $1,212 to $2,851. It is true that in India the fraction of the $1/day poor in the entire population fell from 52 per cent to 34 per cent, but in China that fraction plummeted precipitously from 64 per cent to 10 per cent.

So, growth and poverty experiences have differed. The end result, however, remains that Emerging Asian economic growth, overall, has lifted hundreds of millions of people out of extreme poverty, a striking achievement seen nowhere else in the world in the last quarter of a century.

SOURCES OF GROWTH

How did all this come about?

Different ways are available to break down economic growth into its driving forces. Here it is useful to do the following. Decompose growth into contributions due to physical capital, labour input, and (total factor) productivity or TFP. Physical capital includes two components: first, information and communications technology (ICT) — computers, Internet infrastructure, and so on — and second, non-ICT capital — among other things, machines, buildings, factories, and transport infrastructure. Labour input includes two components: first, labour quantity, i.e., hours employed; and second, labour quality or human capital, i.e., person-specific skills from accumulated schooling. Call TFP what is left over that remains unaccounted for after physical capital and labour input: this might include improvements in the general state of science and engineering or of governance and management practice. For short, think of all these as describing technology and knowledge, generally.

The justification for the preceding growth accounting decomposition is that it describes a production function for the aggregate economy. The decomposition derives, therefore, from consideration of the supply side of the economy: the identification of TFP with technology and knowledge is then particularly apt.

Figure 4.8 shows this production-function growth-accounting decomposition of economic growth over two periods, 1985–95 and 2000–05, across the G7 economies (including Japan) on the one hand, and Emerging Asia on the other. The evidence shows that even in the earlier period TFP contributed significantly to growth in Emerging Asia, indeed by more than twice the rate it did in the G7.[2] However, in the earlier period "mere sweat" certainly did account for a large part of growth in Emerging Asia:

FIGURE 4.8
Demonstration of Economic Growth, 1989–2005

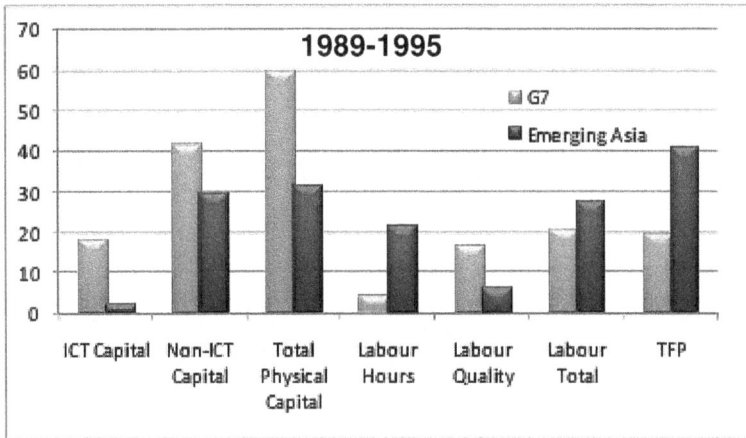

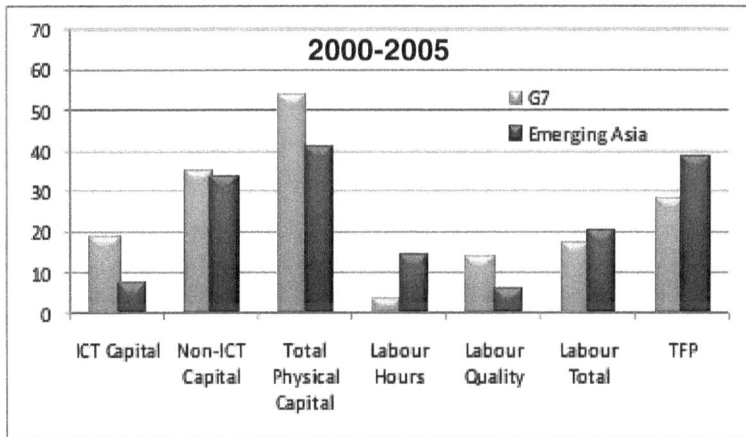

labour hours alone contributed 21.3 per cent, while labour quality
only 6.2 per cent — the total contributed by labour input came
to 27.5 per cent. By contrast, in the later period, labour input's
total contribution came to only 20 per cent, with TFP's hardly
changed but physical capital — and especially ICT capital —
surging to take the lead.

Before 1995, emerging Asia did grow through TFP, even more than the G7 did. But labour hours mattered much more than labour quality. After 2000, physical capital's contribution surged ahead, while TFP's held firm. These numbers are from Jorgensen and Vu (2006).

Emerging Asia transformed from relying overly on labour for growth, to drawing instead on contributions from information and communications technology, while at the same time maintaining high rates of TFP growth.

Just as with poverty reduction, however, this depiction of Emerging Asia comes with important differences across economies. Figure 4.9 shows that for both China and India TFP contribution has remained high throughout 1989–2005. Both China and India, again, drew heavily on labour hours for growth through the mid-1990s. Since then, though, Chinese growth has shifted significantly towards greater reliance on physical capital and drawn much less on the contribution from labour hours. India's profile, however, has remained almost invariant, continuing to rely heavily on labour hours, so that by 2000–05, India was drawing from both labour hours and total labour input twice the contributions that China did. Contrary to the impression of high-tech India given in writings such as Friedman (2006), it is actually India rather than China that has continued to draw growth from intensive use of labour. Just as striking, China has in a relatively short time shifted its engine of growth from labour to capital without compromising TFP's continued contribution.

Figure 4.10 compares the growth experiences of the original East Asian Tigers before and after 1997. Of the four, Taiwan has notably lagged in boosting TFP contribution to economic growth. A similar but muted pattern appears for South Korea. However, both Hong Kong and Singapore have sharply raised their TFP growth contributions to above 40 per cent, a third higher than

FIGURE 4.9
TFP's Contribution for China and India, 1989–2005

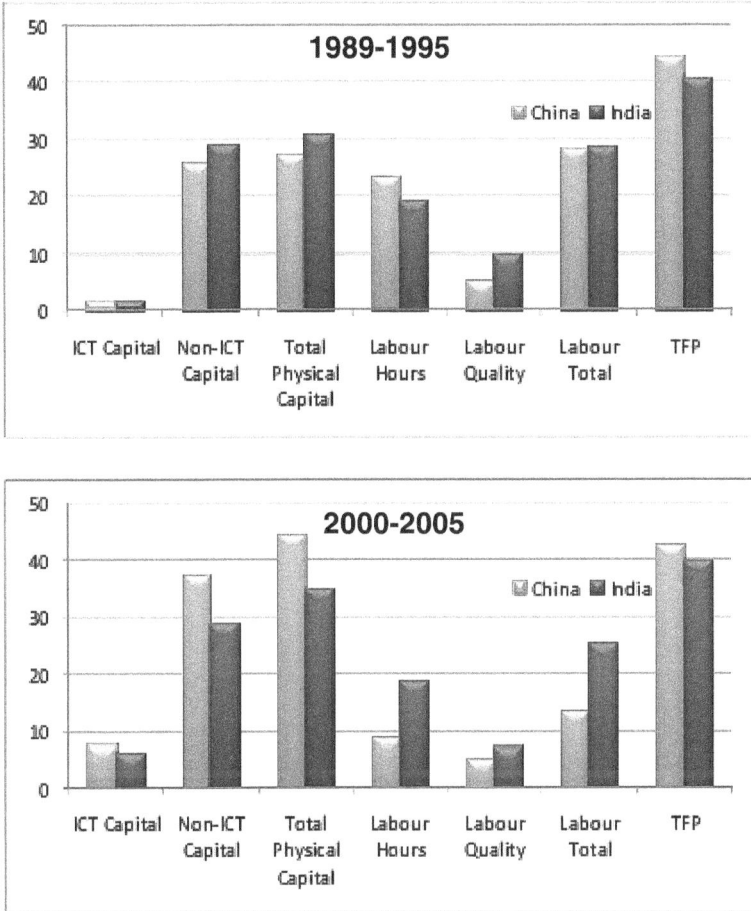

that in the G7 economies. A further striking feature of Singapore's growth is how sharply the economy has reduced its reliance on labour hours, replacing that with continued steady contribution from TFP as well as increased contributions from both ICT and ordinary physical capital.

FIGURE 4.10
TFP's Contribution for East Asian Tigers, 1989–2005

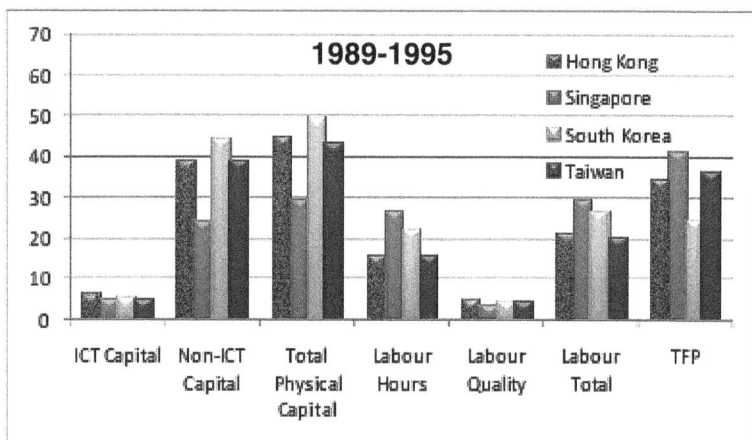

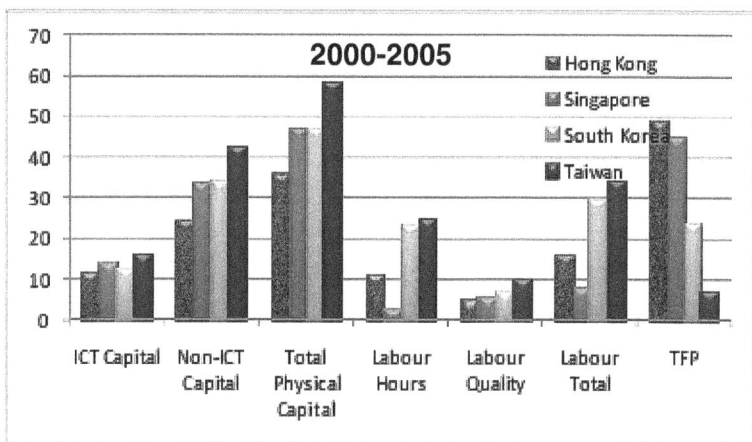

Both China and India drew heavily on labour hours for growth through the mid-1990s. Since then Chinese growth has shifted significantly towards greater reliance on physical capital and much less on labour hours. India's profile, however, has remained almost invariant, relying heavily still on labour hours. TFP contribution has remained high throughout.

Except for Taiwan, the East Asian Tigers have maintained strong growth in TFP throughout. All four have significantly boosted their ICT contribution. Singapore has dramatically reduced its reliance on labour hours.

KNOWLEDGE AND SCHOOLING

TFP incorporates many different possible drivers — in empirical analysis, TFP's contribution to growth is simply what is left over after taking into account labour and capital. Even in its identification as knowledge and technology, the logical distinction of TFP from, say, ICT capital or labour quality is not always obvious. Despite these difficulties, however, the argument is a compelling one that improvements in the state of technology matter critically for sustained growth. And the direction of effects described in the earlier sections is clear.

This section provides related evidence on knowledge — not directly tied to 1997-related developments — but on the output from school systems across economies. Figure 4.11 through Figure 4.13 show results from the OECD's triennial PISA surveys of 15-year-old school children (OECD 2004, 2007). These surveys assess between 4,500 and 10,000 students in each economy, focusing not only on ability to master school curricula but also on useful adult-life mathematical, reading, scientific literacy, and problem-solving skills and knowledge. Although by 2006 the PISA survey covered 57 countries (up from 41 in 2003 and 43 in 2000) it nonetheless omitted some of the economies of interest in this paper.[3] PISA achievement scores range, in effect, from 400 to 600, with the highest countrywide-mean scores typically 560–580. The precise subject focus and scores distributions reported vary through time, thereby restricting some of the description that follows.

Figure 4.11 shows 2003 PISA achievement scores for problem-solving skills, across 15 year-old boys and girls in different economies. The OECD average for boys is 499; that for girls, 501. Hong Kong-China achieved an overall average score of 548, the highest in the survey, but with South Korea, Japan, and Macau-China close behind. Of non-East Asian economies, only Finland, 548; New Zealand, 533 (neither shown); and Canada, 530, achieved average scores 530 or higher.

PISA 2003 — Problem solving skills in 15-year-olds. Boys' scores appear on the vertical axis; girls' scores on the horizontal. The OECD average for boys is 499; that for girls, 501. The highest average score across all economies in the survey is 548 from Hong Kong-China. Data are from OECD (2004).

FIGURE 4.11
PISA Achievement Scores, 2003

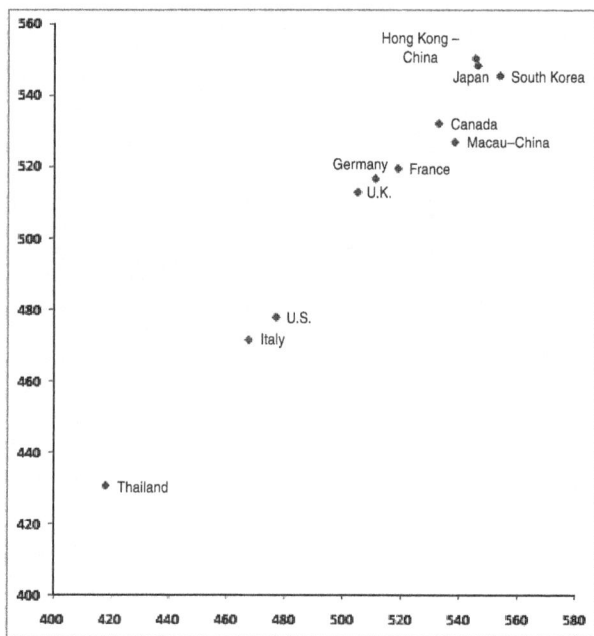

PISA 2006 — Science scores for 15-year-olds. The economy
mean appears on the vertical axis; the percentage reaching the
top two proficiency levels, on the horizontal. For the OECD
overall, the mean is 489 and 9 per cent reach the top two
achievement proficiency levels. The highest mean score was
Finland 563 (not shown). Data are from OECD (2007).

PISA 2006 — Mathematics scores for 15-year-olds. The
economy mean appears on the vertical axis; the percentage
achieving the top two and proficiency levels, on the horizontal.
For the OECD overall, the mean is 484 and 11 per cent reach the
top two achievement proficiency levels. The highest mean score
was Taiwan at 549. Data are from OECD (2007).

Figure 4.12 and Figure 4.13 show results on economy-wide
average and highest within economy achievement from the 2006

FIGURE 4.12
PISA Science Scores, 2006

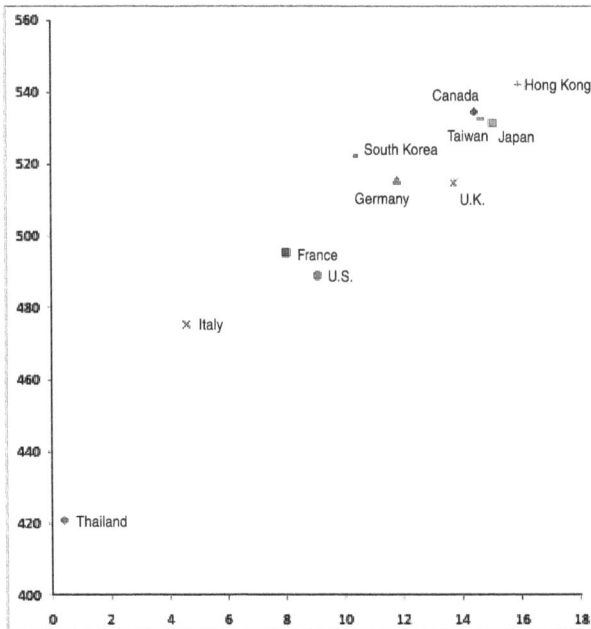

FIGURE 4.13
PISA Mathematics Scores, 2006

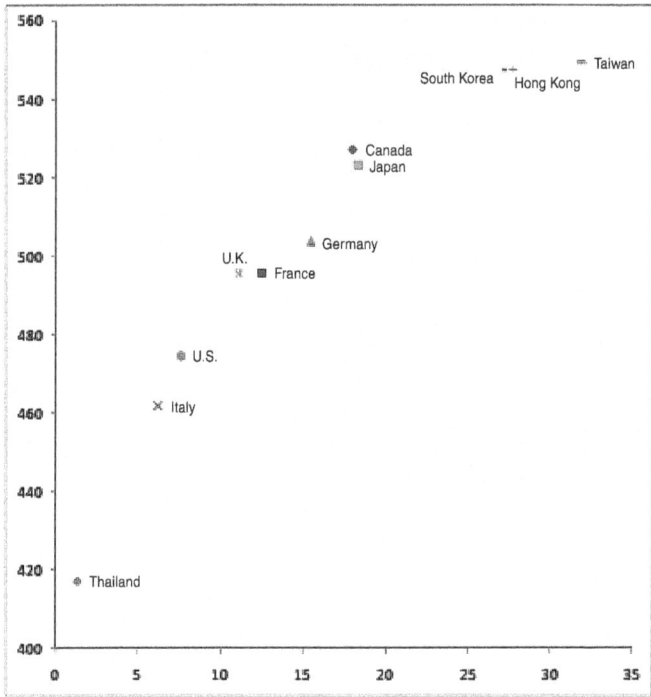

PISA surveys, for science and mathematics across a range of economies.

In Figure 4.12 reporting science achievement, for the OECD overall, the mean is 489 and 49 per cent reach the top two achievement proficiency levels. The highest mean score was Finland 563 (not shown). The four East Asian economies that appear in the sample — Hong Kong, 542; Taiwan, 532; Japan, 531; and South Korea, 522, all rank at the top of the cross-country distribution. Outside of East Asia and Finland, only Canada, 534; Estonia, 531; and New Zealand, 530 (not shown) have mean achievement scores exceeding 530.

In Figure 4.13 reporting mathematics achievement for the OECD overall, the mean is 484 and 11 per cent reach the top two achievement proficiency levels.[4] The highest mean score was Taiwan at 549, with Hong Kong-China and Korea close behind at 547. Of economies not in East Asia, only Finland, 548, and the Netherlands, 531, (neither shown) achieved average scores exceeding 530.

The horizontal axes in both these figures map the percentage of the sample attaining the two highest proficiency levels. The correlation with the mean is strongly positive: The evidence thus shows that the East Asian economies perform well, not just on average, but also have high fractions of top-achievers.

CONCLUSION

A decade ago the East Asian economies were viewed to be catastrophes of financial excess, corporate and political misgovernance, and diminishing returns to over-investment, just as before the 1997 financial crises those same economies were the growth miracles and poster children of managed economic development.

This chapter has presented evidence on how Emerging Asia is freshly restored as the world's economic powerhouse. Its recent success is striking: poverty alleviation in China alone has accounted for 100 per cent of that on the entire Earth. And even if still relatively small in size, Emerging Asia's contribution to world economic growth already matches that of economies many times larger. Along multiple dimensions the world's economic centre of gravity continues to shift east.

What has brought this about? The fundamentals for sustained economic growth include not just good governance and openness to trade, but also creativity and innovation in economic processes:

knowledge and technology. On these latter fronts, the Emerging Asian economies, especially the ones in East Asia, have achieved the highest standards of performance. Some of Emerging Asia does lag but where improvement in schooling and education is needed is also apparent.

Notes

1. The G7 economies, excluding Japan, are Canada, France, Germany, Italy, the U.K., and the U.S. By Emerging Asia I mean Bangladesh, Cambodia, China, Hong Kong, India, Indonesia, Malaysia, Nepal, Pakistan, the Philippines, Singapore, South Korea, Sri Lanka, Taiwan, Thailand, and Vietnam.
2. These numbers are from Jorgensen and Vu (2006). Although those authors used quantities data rather than prices in these calculations, the way I read their findings their results have ended up aligned more in spirit with those of Hsieh (2002) than of Young (1995). Details differ, however, and the greater aggregation levels of concern both here and in Jorgensen and Vu (2006) are not well-compared with the very detailed methodologies of either Hsieh (2002) or Young (1995).
3. In 2009, 67 countries, including Singapore, plan to participate in the PISA survey.
4. At the highest level, the student "can consistently identify, explain, and apply scientific knowledge in a range of complex life situations".

References

Chen, Shaohua and Martin Ravallion. *Absolute Poverty Measures for the Developing World, 1981–2004*. Working Paper, Washington, D.C.: World Bank, 2007.

Friedman, Thomas L. *The World is Flat*. 2nd ed. London: Penguin, 2006.

Hsieh, Chang-tai. "What Explains the Industrial Revolution in East Asia?

Evidence from Factor Markets". *American Economic Review* 92, no. 3 (June 2002): 502–26.

Jorgensen, Dale and Khuong Vu. "Information Technology and the World Economy". In *The Network Society from Knowledge to Policy*, edited by Gustavo Cardoso and Manuel Castells. Washington, D.C., Johns Hopkins University, 2006.

OECD. Programme for International Student Assessment 2003. Paris: OECD, 2004.

———. Programme for International Student Assessment 2006. Paris: OECD, 2007.

World Bank. World Development Indicators Online. Washington, D.C., November 2007.

Young, Alwyn. "The Tyranny of Numbers: Confronting the Statistical Realities of the East Asian Growth Experience". *Quarterly Journal of Economics* 110, no. 3 (August 1995): 641–80.

Chapter 5

COMMERCE VS THE COMMON CONFLICTS OVER THE COMMERCIALISATION OF BIOMEDICAL KNOWLEDGE

Nikolas Rose

INTRODUCTION: GOVERNING A POLITICAL ECONOMY OF HOPE

In many countries, including many Asian countries, the bioeconomy is seen as a crucial economic driver.[1] Singapore, along with countries such as China, Korea and India, is investing heavily in research and development in this area. Indeed since the mid-1980s, Singapore has embraced the ambition of becoming 'Asia's biotech tiger': the Asian focus for the development of the biotechnology industry, with a specific focus on biomedical biotechnology (Ong 2005, p. 341). Singapore has invested heavily in developing in a life science research infrastructure, attracting leading researchers in the life sciences from across the world, setting up education and training programmes to build an indigenous research community, and developing a bioethical governance framework for research and development in the life sciences. By 2003, when Phase 1 of its 'Biopolis' was launched, the biomedical science industry was already contributing S$9.7 billion in manufacturing output and S$6.5 billion in value added, and employing more than 7,000 workers.[2] According to the Deputy Prime Minister, launching what was termed 'the Biopolis of Asia', Biopolis was "the cornerstone of a much broader vision to build up the Biomedical Sciences Industry in Singapore ... to establish the entire value chain of Biomedical Sciences activities in Singapore — from research and development to manufacturing and health care delivery ... [and] to bridge the private sector and public sector research work by creating ... close interface between researchers from industry and scientists from research institutes [that] will accelerate the translation of new discoveries to marketable products".[3]

Singapore is not alone. Across Asia and beyond, governments are pushing for breakthroughs in biomedical research for many reasons, including economic development and competitiveness, scientific prestige, and a patriotic desire to place the nation at the forefront of these crucial developments for human understanding and human health. In this growing and competitive international bioeconomy, the link between health promotion, wealth creation and economic competitiveness underpins the attraction for governments, for venture capitalists, for private foundations, for universities, for researchers, for public funders and for private pressure groups and patient organizations. This is particularly so in age of 'translational medicine'. By translational medicine, I refer to the belief that there is a crucial link between advances in basic biological knowledge of human biology — genetics, neurochemistry, metabolism — and the understanding and effective treatment of diseases ranging from rare genetic conditions such as Huntington's Disease, through common complex disorders such as breast and ovarian cancer and diabetes, through to the diseases of an increasingly aging population such as the dementias. It is this belief, linking together politicians, regulators, researchers, clinicians and actual and potential patients that constitutes what has been termed 'a political economy of hope' (Novas 2006; Rose 2006).

But the hopes for health and wealth that are invested in biomedical knowledge and its potential products create both pressures and downsides. Indeed I have just come to Singapore from an international conference in China organised by BIONET — a network that I coordinate from LSE which consists of twenty partners from Europe and China — basic biomedical researchers, clinicians, bioethicists, political scientists, sociologists, anthropologists, lawyers and representatives of industry — exploring the regulatory challenges that such developments are producing, especially in the context of growing international collaboration and competition.[4] Recently, we have become painfully aware of the problems that can be generated by the pressure on researchers to generate findings with economic and biomedical benefits, through the Korean case of Professor Hwang and his false claims of creation of human embryonic stem cell lines (Gottweis and Triendl 2006). However scientific fraud is not my focus today. Instead I want to explore some of the tensions for knowledge producers in the novel relations between health and wealth in what has come to be termed, in Europe, the 'knowledge based bioeconomy'.

SCIENCE — BUSINESS OR VOCATION?

Let me begin by framing my remarks between two quotes. In September 2003 the Danish Minister for Research and Innovation, published a new action plan for Danish universities that aimed to create incentives to strengthen cooperation between universities and the business sector so that universities would undertake the research that the business sector needs. I cite this among many similar efforts in other countries because its title was so frank: 'New roads between research and business — *from thought to invoice.*' ('Fra tanke til faktura') (my emphasis). Almost half a century earlier, in April 1955, on the day after the announcement that the polio vaccine he had developed was safe and effective, Jonas Salk was asked by Edward R. Murrow on U.S. national TV, who owned the patent. Salk answered 'Well, the people I would say. There is no patent. Could you patent the sun?' (Smith 1990).[5]

Salk's benign sense that the knowledge that he had helped create, or to be more precise the intervention that was derived from it, should belong to the people, fitted within a long tradition of scientific knowledge as open, public, freely available to all, independent of self interest. The acceptance of scientific knowledge claims has long depended on their 'public' nature, although this has, of course, been generated by many different 'technologies of trust'. As Steven Shapin has shown, in his *Social History of Truth*, in seventeenth-century Europe, a claim to truth had to be guaranteed by demonstration of an experiment in front of reliable and honourable witnesses, who would testify about their experience in front of others (Shapin 1994). As scientific practice developed over the decades that followed, this background of trust was crucial to the organized and focussed scepticism that became the hallmark of scientific investigation. Perhaps things began to change in Europe and North America in the late nineteenth century. Max Weber's famous lecture of 1918, 'Science as a Vocation', was given when the very nature of scientific research was altering, as it was professionalised both within the universities and in industry (Weber 2004). As those activities we now call science proliferated over the twentieth century, scientific integrity was to be assured by a belief in the integrity of individual scientists and of the scientific establishment, in their commitment to principles of honesty and reliability in reporting the results of experiments, in criteria of reproducibility — the demand that results be 'replicated' — and in the constraints of the peer review process required before publication: for publication — placing your arguments and claims in the public domain — constituted 'the scientific commons' — in principle available to all.

Of course, sociological research on actual scientific communities has shown that, in their everyday practices, scientists themselves are subject to the same pressures, aspirations and dilemmas as any other group, beset by passions and desires, and by emotions of ambition, loyalty and rivalry. We know that the acceptance of some claims as facts rather than others is the outcome of complicated social processes of persuasion (Latour 1987). And Murrow's 1955 reference to a patent showed that, even while knowledge might be freely available to all, the inventions that are fruits of that knowledge have long been transformed into property (MacLeod 1988). But developments over the last decades of the twentieth century threw these issues into sharp focus, and, for some, radically changed the character of what would count as scientific truth and the way in which its benefits might become available. Here I will focus on the field of biomedicine, its location within a growing global bioeconomy, and in particular on the new relations between biomedical knowledge production and its capitalisation.

Historians of biology have argued convincingly that from about the 1930s in Europe, when it comes to knowledge of life, biology moved from an era of representation to one of intervention — intervention was not only vital to the process of discovery, but the hope that biological discoveries would enable effective intervention into the living world in order to produce human benefits — whether in agriculture, in industry or in biomedicine — became part of the telos of biology itself (Kay 1993; Rheinberger 1997; Rheinberger 2000). Biological truth is thus 'path dependent' — this is so even for basic biological knowledge, but it is more so in the fusion of biology and medicine that, since the 1960s, has been termed biomedicine (Rose 2001; Rose 2006). And a key driver in the development of knowledge of human life are the beliefs held by all involved in what might potentially be done with that knowledge — what it might produce, in terms of both health and wealth. It is that link between health and wealth, between virtue and profit, that is driving the expanding biomedical bioeconomy. It underpins its attraction for governments, venture capitalists, private foundations, for universities and researchers and for public funders in age of translational medicine with its emphasis on the importance of the move from bench to bedside, from scientific discovery to clinical — and economic — pay-off.

After a gloomy time in the early years of this century, following the burst of what is now termed 'the genomics bubble' — of which more later — hopes in the potential of the global biotechnology industry have started to recover across the globe, driven in large part by the biomedical sector: in 2006 the global biotech industry was estimated to have a value of US$73,470,000,000, of which 75 per cent was located in the U.S., 15 per cent in Europe, about 4.5 per cent in Canada and 4.5 per cent in the Asia-Pacific region (Ernst & Young 2007, p. 7). As I have already noted, the intense international competition in this area generates pressure on researchers that, without appropriate controls and governance, can lead to the kind of scientific fraud that we saw in Korea, with Professor Hwang. But it also generates some other problems, and I want to explore some of these in what follows.

The intense capitalisation of medicine has been much criticised in some areas, notably where it is most evident — for where it leads to the sale of bodily components, organs, embryos, eggs, sperm.... (Scheper-Hughes 2000; Scheper Hughes and Waquant 2002). But, away from such clearly problematic areas, critical attention has recently been directed to the ways in which this capitalisation is reshaping very heartlands of biomedical research — the corporatisation of science and the universities. Some term this corporatisation, that is to say the links between the academy and industry, an 'enclosure of the commons' — a reference to those earlier enclosures of land and its bounties, when common ground that had been available to all for grazing and hunting was transformed into private property (Boyle 2003). In the U.S., many have commented on the impact of the 1980 Bayh-Dole Amendments, which, for the first time, gave up federal rights to intellectual property resulting from research supported from government funds, allowing those property rights and the value that might flow from them to be claimed by universities or by individual scientists (Kennedy 2001). The ostensible aim was to avoid important scientific discoveries lying idle, and not contributing to national well being. But this act, coupled with other legal changes, opened biomedical research to a flood of private investment and venture capital.

Trends in the U.S. were followed across much of the rest of the world, and the new opportunities were embraced enthusiastically by research universities, who set up technology transfer offices, participated in start-up companies, and entered into the murky world of patenting, licensing, distribution of royalties, and complex commercial relations with the corporate world. On the one hand, this brought new funds, facilities, faculty and opportunities to biomedical research and those who engaged in it. For example, according to the U.S. Association of University Technology Managers Report in 2006, $45 billion in R&D expenditures were received by U.S. academic centres in that year alone, 697 new products were introduced into the market, and as a result of these relations between industry and the academy, a total of 4,350 new products were introduced from Financial Year 98 through Financial Year 06 and 12,672 licenses and options were managed, each yielding active income to a university, hospital or research centre; over the quarter of a century since the passage of Bayh-Dole, U.S. universities have launched 5,724 spinout companies (Association of University Technology Managers 2007).[6]

On the other hand, many argued that the principles that should govern scientific knowledge were being compromised by the drive for intellectual property and the growing entanglements between universities, researchers, industry and knowledge claims. This has not just been a concern of academic critics. For example in 2002, the Royal Society of London set up a study to ask 'whether the use of laws which encourage the commercial exploitation of scientific research is helping or hindering progress in fields such as genetics'. Its study 'has been set up in response to concerns about how best to protect the ownership of inventions, through patents for instance, while preserving a free exchange of ideas and knowledge between researchers'. The Chair, Professor Roger Needham, said: 'Science thrives on discovery and the rapid spread of knowledge, so it is important that the flow of information between researchers is not choked off by the secrecy required, for instance, before a patent is filed.' Particular attention was to be paid to whether 'patenting of genes could permit monopolies for health treatments by undeserving enterprises that have merely discovered the information rather than produced cures. We need laws that encourage investment in the science, but which allow as many people as possible to share the benefits.'

The conclusion of its study was that 'Intellectual property rights (IPRs) can stimulate innovation by protecting creative work and investment, and by encouraging the ordered exploitation of scientific discoveries for the good of society. ... [But] the fact that they are monopolies can cause a tension between private profit and public good. Not least, they can hinder the free exchange of ideas and information on which science thrives. ...'[7] It argued that while patents can provide protection for inventions, they can limit competition, especially where they are broad in scope, making it impracticable for others to pursue research in areas claimed by patents, and encouraging a climate of secrecy to ensure that the patent is granted before an idea reaches the public domain, hindering the free flow of ideas on which scientific progress depends.

In our area of biomedical biotechnology, I only have time to discuss two sets of questions. Of course, some have what one might term 'fundamentalist' objections to 'the commoditisation of life' arguing that some things — notably the human body and its components, including organs, reproductive components, and genes — by their very nature, should be outside the property system. Sometimes this is because of what Leon Kass would term 'the wisdom of repugnance' — the very idea offends 'our gut instincts' (Kass 1997). Sometimes it is because some things are thought to be 'beyond property' because they are the creation of god, part of an uncommodifiable nature, or belong to the common heritage of humanity. But here I want to look at some specific concerns.

GENE PATENTING

The question of whether there can be, or should be property in human body parts is complex and controversial. While the illicit trade in organs is widespread, in Europe, the U.S., and most Asian countries, people are forbidden to sell their own body parts, with some exceptions (e.g. blood in the USA) (Scott 1981). In biomedicine, the famous John Moore case, which I will not discuss here, raised the issue of whether cell lines derived from body can be private property and if so, who may own them — the person from whom they were derived, the doctors, the researchers, the hospital.... (Gold 1996) The issue is particularly difficult in case of ownership of 'genes', for what is at stake here lies somewhere between matter (the actual DNA) and information (the knowledge of the DNA sequence) (Parry 2004).

A further question is whether one might patent a gene sequence that one has simply 'discovered' the sequence of DNA bases that code for protein — or if this violates the ancient Lockeian principle that property rights refer to fruits of labour, an option only available when an individual has mixed his or her labour with a natural resource, not in the resource itself. Various organizations have applied this principle to the Human Genome, suggesting that the sequence itself should not be patentable. UNESCO combines this Lockeian objection with a fundamentalist one, when it states that: 'the Human Genome underlies that fundamental unity of all members of the human family... The Human Genome in its natural state shall not give rise to financial gain.'[8] But what is 'in its natural state?'

U.S. patenting law initially addressed the issue of patenting entities that had an altered genetic complement in the 1930s in relation to plant breeding. They eventually allowed plant breeders to patent the new varieties of plant they had produced, partly on an analogy with patenting products of chemical processes, but more significantly because they considered breeders to be inventors because they used methodical techniques of research and experimentation (Demaine and Fellmeth 2002).[9] But the first test in relation to contemporary genomics came in the

1970s, in relation to an attempt by Ananda Chakrabarty to patent a transgenic oil-eating bacterium that he had produced by recombinant DNA technology and which might have value in treating oil spills. The patent was initially rejected by the patent examiner on the grounds that living things were not patentable, and eventually went to the Supreme Court in the famous case of Diamond vs. Chakrabarty. The patent was finally approved in 1980 on the grounds that whether alive or dead, the bacterium was not a product of nature but of Chakrabarty and hence was patentable subject matter. In another controversial case, in 1984, an application was filed in the U.S. for a patent on a transgenic animal — Harvard's OncoMouse — and initially granted. It led to a flood of objections — partly economic — about fostering monopolies — and partly moral — life had a sacred or vital property, was not a mere arrangement of chemicals, and so should not be subject to patent. However the patent was grated. And in a 1987 case concerning oyster breeding, U.S. Board of Patent Appeals and Interferences ruled that patents could in principle be granted on living animals but not on human beings.

Things were different in Europe, partly because of the nature of the European patent system which allows third parties to contest the validity of patents. After initially granting the patent to Harvard's OncoMouse, on appeal from a whole range of political parties, NGOs, religious and other sources, the European Patent Office (EPO) rejected the application, not because it violated Article 53(a) of European Patent Convention — the public order and morality clause — but because it violated Article 53 (b) which prohibits patenting plant or animal varieties or anything produced by a natural biological process, except microbiological products. In 2001, after appeal from Harvard, it approved a patent limited to transgenic mice containing an additional cancer gene — a ruling that was finally upheld in 2005. And despite these controversies, over the last two decades of the twentieth century, over 15,000 patents in the field of biotechnology were filed by the European Patent office, of which about a third were in the area of genetics, and half of these were for DNA sequences isolated from human genetic material.

The issue remains controversial, not only in genomics but in other biomedical areas. An ongoing area which I cannot discuss here, concerns patents on stem cells — notably the much disputed 'Edinburgh' patent with the title 'Isolation, selection and propagation of animal transgenic stem cells' which describes a method of using genetic engineering to isolate stem cells — including embryonic stem cells — from more differentiated cells in a cell culture in order to obtain pure stem cell cultures — the grant of the patent led to fierce protests and triggered a major public debate on the patenting of stem-cell technology which centred on whether the patent extended to the isolation of human stem cells. In 2002, the patent was maintained in an amended form that no longer includes human or animal *embryonic* stem cells, but still covers modified human and animal stem cells other than embryonic stem cells; it was the subject of further appeals which were finally withdrawn in 2007.[10]

As far as genes are concerned, the issue came to a head at the turn of the century, in the dispute between Craig Venter of Celera Genomics, and the publicly funded Human Genome Project, led, in the later stages, by the U.K. based Wellcome Trust and their principal investigator, John Sulston. In 1991 Venter applied for patents on 315 'expressed sequence tags' (ESTs) — coded sequences derived from random fragments of DNA (cDNA) — *and* the genes they came from. This failed on technical grounds — because ESTs did not fully characterise genes — but it led to a public debate in the USA on the patenting of genes. Some objected because patents on DNA sequences alone — 'genes' — would not fulfil the basic requirements of a patent — novelty, non-obviousness and utility. Yet initially the U.S. patent system did allow patenting a DNA sequence without any knowledge of its functions.[11]

In Celera Genomics Venter developed a powerful method of gene sequencing, which he applied to the human genome, with the intention of patenting the genes he discovered, by linking these sequences to their functions. The publicly funded Human Genome Project, led by the Wellcome Trust sought to prevent this, and to put the sequence map of genes into the public domain. After intervention from Bill Clinton and Tony Blair, the two teams sequencing the human genome agreed to announce their rival maps of over 90 per cent of the human genome on the same day 11 February 2001. Venter's team published in *Science* — providing only limited free access to the full raw sequence data — and the Wellcome team published in *Nature* — with full access to the sequence data (Lander, Linton et al. 2001; Venter, Adams et al. 2001). Just before this happened, in January 2001, the U.S. Patent Office issued new guidelines: companies may indeed patent genes or even pieces of genes if they are associated with a specific use, such as the development of a disease. Together with previous case law, this has led to a situation where a gene can be patented, but only if it has been cloned in the laboratory, its function defined, and it can be shown that it meets a three-prong test of utility — that is, having specific, credible and substantial uses. Raw DNA sequence data would not be patentable by itself, but an excised gene is eligible for a patent as a composition of matter or as an article of manufacture because that DNA molecule does not occur in that isolated form in nature. Synthetic DNA preparations are eligible for patents because their purified state is different from the naturally occurring compound.

Let us move forward seven years to 2008. The publicly funded Human Genome Programme has put all of its information on the genetic sequence of human beings on the web, available to all, and has continued to update and complete it: thus the sequence itself is in the public domain and cannot be patented. Also in the public domain are many 'genes' — that is to say the information that links parts of the sequences with specified proteins — which have been lodged by researchers in various publicly available databases. So what remains to be patented? Well, there are still some controversial areas where patenting of sequence data can occur — for example in the U.S., there is controversy over precisely how high a barrier the 'inventive step' and 'utility' thresholds should be (Davis and Kelley et al. 2005), and in Europe the sequence itself can effectively be monopolised through a patent which is framed as an 'application of a discovery' supported by claiming differences between what is being patented and what is in the public domain.[12] But perhaps more generally, the focus is now not so much on the sequence itself, but on the function of the sequence, the consequences of small anomalies or variations in that sequence, the means of identifying the particular version of it that is possessed by any individual (genetic tests), and the clinical uses of it. This is the new field of contest over patents on life.

Why should one be concerned about such patents? Let me list FOUR key reasons that have been given by critics: each deserves a fuller discussion and evaluation than I can provide here.

First, what James Boyle (2003) calls 'the right of sources'. That is to say the argument that as genetic information comes from a source, that source — whether individual or group — should retain some rights in it or in the profits made from it. In biomedicine the discovery of the gene sequence for a disease depends on the donation of samples from families who are afflicted by the condition together with medical records and genealogical information. In some case this has led to demands for 'benefit sharing' with the 'community' — perhaps a population with a high prevalence of that disorder, perhaps a group of families with large numbers of affected members.[13] In more radical instances, it has led to the families themselves — those who have donated the samples — forming corporations that then issue patents to secure intellectual property in their own disease genes, in order to ensure that those sufferers themselves benefits from the results of the research (Rapp and Taussig et al. 2002; Taussig and Heath et al. 2003; Heath and Rapp et al. 2004). But obviously this strategy is not available to all. In particular, where research on the genomics of disease is undertaken by researchers from developed countries using populations from less developed countries, patenting creates an imbalance. This arises from the disparity between the location of those who have contributed the samples, and the location in the global bioeconomy where the patents are held and where those who benefit reside — normally, of course, while the subjects or donors may be based in China, Mexico or India, the patents are held by multinationals based in the U.S. or Europe and the benefits — and often the drugs themselves — flow to those in these regions.

Second, anti-commons. The patenting of a gene sequence may hamper or event prevent others from working on it, even when the owner does not consider it worth pursuing, thus blocking potential lines of discovery. For example Harvard University owns the patent on the 'Nuclear Factor kappa B' family of transcription factors, along with MIT and the Whitehead Institute. This is a family of proteins that regulate the expression of many genes, including those thought to be involved in many diseases. Harvard licensed the patent exclusively to Ariad Pharmaceuticals, which claims rights over 'all future inventions that will be made or discovered that operate on the biological principle of the NF-kb pathway' (Ready 2003, quoted by Triggle 2004, p. 143). In May 2006 a federal jury ruled that Eli Lilly & Company had infringed this patent in developing two drugs — for osteoporosis and for septic shock — because these drugs worked on this basic pathway. They ordered Lilly to pay US$65.2 million dollars in back royalties to Ariad. According to the New York Times of 9 May 2006 'Lilly argued in the trial that Ariad's patent covered a natural phenomenon and was therefore invalid.' And Lilly's General Council argued 'The Ariad position is equivalent to discovering that gravity is the force that makes water run downhill and then demanding the owners of all the existing hydroelectric plants begin to pay patent royalties on their use of gravity.'[14] Ariad had not developed any drugs itself, but wanted to sell licences to all companies and researchers who sought to work on this pathway, although as of 2006 no company had agreed to pay for such a licence. Another biotech firm, Amgen, is in legal battle with Ariad, seeking to protect its arthritis drug Enbrel from infringement charges. However this is not simply a battle of the corporations, the scientists who discovered the drug include two Nobel Laureates, Phillip A. Sharp and David Baltimore — according to an article in *Nature* they declined to comment on the case (Ready 2002).

Third, patenting a gene sequence together with a test to identify disease related variants. The most controversial example was Myriad Genetics who, in the U.S. and Canada in 2000 and 2001 patented a test (BRCAnalysis) for two of the sequences associated with a higher risk of developing hereditary breast cancer, BRCA1 and BRCA2. Any individual, doctor or researcher who wanted to use test for these variants was required to do so through Myriad, and had to pay a fee of around US$3,000. The American College of

Medical Genetics stated its concern that giving such monopoly rights would limit the accessibility of competitively priced genetic testing services, hinder the development of quality assurance programmes and impede the scope and pace of research that might have a beneficial clinical impact. Others, for example the Institut Curie in France, expressed the concern that commercial ambitions were leading Myriad to overemphasise the accuracy and predictive value of their test. Indeed, errors were discovered in the Myriad sequence and by the time they were corrected, the accurate sequence was already in the public domain: for this and other reasons the patent was struck down by European Patent Office.[15] In practice, Myriad's patent was widely ignored, despite the fact that they issued many 'cease and desist' notices. Public health bodies in many regions argued against the wide use of such tests in non-symptomatic individuals. However, Myriad is now engaged in an intensive direct-to-consumer marketing campaign for their tests. This is just one of a stream of genetic tests coming onto the market, not linked to patents on the genes themselves, but claiming patents in their capacity to identify the particular sequences that may be linked to susceptibility for a disease or medical condition.

This is the growing area of 'personal genomics' (McGuire and Cho et al. 2007; Jordan 2008; McGuire and Caulfield et al. 2008). Given the relative failure of business models based on finding genes of major effect for common complex disorders, and the slump in share value of corporations who based their business models on such hopes — the burst of the genomics bubble that I mentioned earlier — commercial genomics organizations are now not only marketing to providers but are seeking to appeal directly to the consumer. Multiple sites — for example decodeme.com and 23andme.com — are springing up offering a direct-to-consumer commercial service costing between US$950 and US$2,500, in which, individuals supply a saliva sample, and the company provides information on 'their personal disease risk' — using algorithms derived from a new form of genomic research known as 'genome wide association studies'. As many have argued, the medical relevance of such information for treatment or prevention is small, yet the individual and social downsides are potentially great, running from genetic discrimination in insurance, to the promotion of non-proven interventions in relation to very small variations in risk, and, not least, to the exacerbation of fears about risk in the worried well (Pearson and Manolio 2008). Privatisation, marketization and consumerization of genomic information on disease risk is certainly not a public good.

Fourth, patenting leads to a rush to translation. That is to say, patenting gives an incentive to commercialise the discovery and take the product to the market in order to recoup the initial costs of the research and to generate profit before the patent expires, irrespective of wider social concerns. One area where one sees this is in pharmacogenomics — the attempt to 'personalise' drug therapies by matching drugs to genetic information on their efficacy and safety — which varies from individual to individual, and also varies between 'population groups' (Davies 2006). This is an area of great controversy as it raises the prospect of re-differentiating the human species genetically along population lines in the name of effective therapy (Goldstein and Hirschhorn 2004; Tate and Goldstein 2004). There are many drivers of pharmacogenomics — targeting may help drugs get to market more quickly, may enable researchers to reduce the size of clinical trial populations, may restrict the incidence of damaging side-effects that lead to licensing failure and so forth — facilitating the path from bench to bedside. On the other hand we can already observe pharmaceutical companies obtaining licences for drugs, for example for the treatment of many cancers, on the condition that they are prescribed only on the basis of genetic tests — and both the patent on the drug and the patent on the test are owned by the corporation in question, thus making their availability dependent on the ability of an individual or a health insurance system to pay and displacing the cheaper generic alternatives. The public consequences of this move are not yet clear. It is a difficult matter to evaluate the balance between more effective targeting of expensive drug treatments, increased health service costs, and, of course, increased health inequalities. And this is exacerbated by the fact that there are few incentives for corporations to invest in the pharmacogenomic research that would increase the efficacy of drugs for those in population groups who do not have the resources to pay for them.

DEVELOPMENT OF PHARMACEUTICALS

This discussion of genetics has already led me to a second issue, which relates to pharmaceuticals.

Of course, pharmaceutical companies have become a popular villain (Angell 2004; Healy 2004; Moynihan and Cassels 2005). But we should recall that many effective drugs have only come to market because such companies have been prepared to invest risk capital over long periods to develop them — even if they have, in many cases, relied on basic research undertaken in publicly funded laboratories. Drug companies themselves are increasingly striving to represent themselves as good global citizens and emphasise their corporate social responsibility, although some have been highly critical of these endeavours (Elliot 2001; Elliot 2004; Novas 2006). Yet however disingenuous this may be in some cases, their very existence suggests that it is no longer sufficient for those in the pharmaceutical industry to assert that their responsibilities as corporations are solely to their shareholders. Patents and high costs of patented drugs may be necessary compensation, important incentives, and legitimate rewards for such work in the name of public good (Relman and Angell 2002). This is not the place to rehearse the argument about the implications of the high costs of such drugs for the less developed world, important as that is. Rather, let me just enumerate some more general downsides of the dependence of drug development and production on commercial corporations and market mechanisms.[16]

First, evidence and efficacy. In almost all regions of the world, drugs can only be licensed for the market if they meet certain conditions set by regulatory bodies, such as the U.S. Food and Drug Administration (FDA) or the Medicines and Healthcare Regulatory Authority (MHRA) in the U.K. (Wahlberg and McGoey 2007). Such bodies developed over the 20th century in response to numerous pressures and some disastrous consequences of poorly tested and dangerous medications. They depend for their licensing decisions on data provided to them by the companies themselves, who carry out the testing of their drugs through the various phases of the process. Today the so called 'gold standard' is the randomized clinical trial, in which the efficacy of a drug is tested, against either a placebo or another drug (so called Treatment as Usual). The results of several such trials are combined together to enable a judgement to be made as to whether the benefits of the drug are significant and outweigh any risks of side effects. However commercial pressures to bring the drug though the licensing system generate many problems.

Second, selective reporting. Companies are not legally required to submit evidence from all trials they have conducted, and many trials that give ambiguous or negative results are not published, skewing risk-benefit calculations. This issue recently came to the fore in U.K. debates about guidelines for the use of a particular class of anti-depressant drugs for children — the SSRIs or selective serotonin re-uptake inhibitors. While the published data indicated that the benefits of these drugs outweighed any risks, those evaluating these drugs belatedly discovered unpublished trial data held by the pharmaceutical companies; when they recalculated risk-benefit ratios including these data the picture changed, and they advised against the use of most members of this class of drugs for children (Whittington and Kendall et al. 2004, 2005; Kendall and McGoey 2007).

Third, publication bias. Analyses clearly show that drug trials published in the scientific journals that have been carried out or funded by the pharmaceutical companies report higher levels of efficacy and lower levels of unwanted effects or adverse incidents than those carried out by independent researchers. Yet many trials undertaken by university based researchers are funded by industry, and indeed such industry funding has long been an important source of income for biomedical researchers in universities, especially in the U.S. While there are clear guidelines as to how such university-industry relations should be established, a number of recent surveys have drawn attention to the extent to which they are not adhered to, notably where the drug company funding the research uses confidentiality or other agreement to prevent unfavourable results being published, or to sue those researchers who do publish such results (several of these are discussed in Triggle 2004).

Fourth, corporate capture. Over and above these individual conflicts, there are other actual or perceived conflicts where universities or departments have more general financial links with biotech companies, either in the form of gifts, or more specific agreements. For example in the celebrated Berkeley-Novartis deal, a pharmaceutical company, Novartis, gave UC Berkeley $25 million over five years, in exchange for the first rights to license any discovery that was made on the basis of research that was supported by Novartis funds; critics of such arrangements within the University were reported to have suffered various forms of disadvantage, including in relation to tenure processes (Triggle 2004, p. 144).

Fifth, conflict of interests. Even where specific malpractice has not been identified, many critics have expressed concern about the fact that some leading researchers on the efficacy of pharmaceuticals, who often sit on the regulatory bodies that are involved in the licensing process such as the FDA and the MHRA, have financial links with the companies whose products they are evaluating (Healy 2004). It is notable that bodies such as the National Institute of Health have recently begun to address this issue.[17] Further, the scientific and medical journals have, over the last few years, greatly increased their vigilance on this issue, requiring much clearer statements of conflicts of interest to be published along with reports of studies, and using the mechanism of publicity to address the problem that such relations between commerce and science raise for the issue of trust in knowledge with which I began. I will return to the question of trust in my conclusion.

Sixth, outsourcing of trials. The increased costs of clinical trials, and the search for 'drug naïve' populations on which to carry out the trials, coupled with the outsourcing of many clinical trials to commercial 'contract research organizations' has led to numerous trials of drugs for western pharmaceutical companies being undertaken in less developed regions — where people can be recruited more cheaply, ethical barriers are easier to surmount, and the actual labour of the trial can be done by local researchers at a fraction of the costs (Abraham 2007). This is generating a number of problems (Petryna 2005; Petryna and Lakoff et al. 2006; Petryna 2007). There is, of course, frank corruption: financial inducements to doctors and researchers to conduct the trial and even to generate favourable results for the trial company. But perhaps more serious is the paradoxical fact that the drugs are often under trial for conditions that are not the major public health problems in those countries where the trials are carried out, and the drugs that will be produced as a result will not be available to those populations — the benefits will be transported to the more developed world and the drugs will be too expensive to afford in the countries where they were trialled.

Once more, we can see that the drive to patent and to commercialise leads to priority being given to the development of those products that will meet the demands of those who have both the willingness and the ability to pay. As James Boyle puts it: 'to have a patent-driven drug policy is to *choose* to deliver lots of drugs that deal with male-pattern baldness, but also with real and important diseases: rheumatoid arthritis, various cancers and heart disease. It is to choose *not* to have a system that delivers drugs for tropical diseases, or indeed for any disease which is suffered overwhelmingly by the national or global poor' (Boyle 2003, pp. 20–21).

CONCLUSION

These issues are, of course, not new. But they are given added salience by the intense contemporary capitalization of health, disease and biomedicine, and by global competition in 'the knowledge based bioeconomy'. How then can the intellectual property system be aligned with incentives for the public good and for global justice?

James Boyle has argued that we need a new way of evaluating our whole innovation system to measure 'our system of current innovation against one that, in questions of basic human need, such as access to essential medicines, stipulated a certain minimum valuation to human life, even among the global poor' and he proposes solutions to the failures and inefficiencies of our current intellectual property system 'ranging from supplementing the patent system with government bounties or prizes, to offering dual zone patents, to directly subsidizing research' (Boyle 2003, p. 17). He suggests innovations such as an intellectual property ombudsman to represent the interests of the public and the public domain in relation to patent applications. And he argues for interdisciplinary scholarship — between legal scholars, economists and social scientists that can engage in this encounter with the claims of distributive justice and human rights, and devise ways — and there are already some very good examples — of modulating the costs and incentives of the relations between commerce and the commons in this desired direction. Whatever the merits of these specific proposals, it is clear that the issues that he and others have raised highlight crucial challenges, for academics, for universities, for regulators and for all those concerned with the significance of biomedicine and health in strategies for global justice.

I would like to end by returning very briefly to the question of trust. Steven Shapin, in his social history of truth, argued that science has become a system of knowledge only through its constitution, in various ways, as a system of trusting persons (Shapin 1994). That dependence on trust runs throughout — from trust in the reagents and instruments used in an experiment, the statistical procedures and computer programmes used to analyse them, in the organization of laboratory and research groups, in the truthfulness of the reporting of the results, in the scrutiny exercised in the process of publication, and in the rigour of public evaluation by peers and others.[18] Trust, then, has an ineradicable role, even in the most empirical forms of scientific knowledge. Scientists have to trust a great deal if they are to be able to direct their sceptical enquiries to a specific site or question — for this background knowledge has to be taken as a collective and trustworthy ground for their own specific research. And over and beyond the trust that makes the scientific activity possible, there a further question for non-scientists. In our own times, where we are faced with multiple authorities, each of whom has multiple critics, who are we to trust to give us information, advice, diagnosis and effective treatments in those most fundamental situations where our very body and mortality is at stake. The multiple conflicts between commerce and the commons that I have sketched here need to be controlled, managed, governed and redirected if, in our global and unjust world, trust in biomedical knowledge is legitimately to be regained.

Notes

1. Thanks to Alain Pottage and Siva Thambisetty for reading a draft of this chapter and helping me avoid too many errors on intellectual property; thanks also to my discussants at the Asia Forum for their thoughtful comments. I would like to acknowledge David Triggle's excellent paper, cited in note 3 below, and the writings of James Boyle, which I have drawn upon extensively in what follows. None of them are responsible for my interpretations of their wise advice, or for my mistakes!

2. <http://www.biomedsingapore.com/bms/sg/en_uk/index/newsroom/speeches/2003/laun ch_of_biopolis.html>.

3. The transcript of the speech is at <http://www.biomed-singapore.com/bms/sg/en_uk /index/newsroom/speeches/2003/launch_of_biopolis.html>; since that time Biopolis Phase 2 has been opened in 2006,

with specific new foci in neurosciences and immunology, and Phase 3 is planned for 2009 to support world class research programmes in clinical and translational medicine — see <http://www.one-north.sg/hubs_biopolis.aspx>.

4. For details, see <www.bionet-china.org>.

5. Quoted from D. J. Triggle, "Patenting the Sun: Enclosing the Scientific Commons and Transforming the University — Ethical Concerns", *Drug Development Research* 63, no. 3 (2004): 139–49, at p. 139. The clip from the Murrow interview is available on YouTube at <http://www.youtube.com/watch?v=QHGKLbDt_2Q&eurl=http://www.michaelmoore.com/sicko/dvd/extras.html>.

6. Available at <http://www.autm.net/about/dsp.Detail.cfm?pid=215>.

7. Quoted from their Press Release of 29 August 2002 available at <http://royalsociety.org/news.asp?id=2507>. The report published in 2003 concluded that 'Intellectual property rights (IPRs) can stimulate innovation by protecting creative work and investment, and by encouraging the ordered exploitation of scientific discoveries for the good of society. Although IPRs can aid the conversion of good science to tangible benefits, the fact that they are monopolies can cause a tension between private profit and public good. Not least, they can hinder the free exchange of ideas and information on which science thrives. ... A narrow focus on research most likely to lead directly to IPRs would damage the health of science in the longer term. Moreover, the net income to the Science Base institutions from IPRs coming directly from publicly funded research is unlikely to be a significant fraction of their total. It is therefore important to ensure that intellectual property (IP) policies on protection and exploitation do not have significant negative effects on the direction or the value of Science Base research. The evidence received during our study indicates that patenting rarely delays publication significantly, but that it can encourage a climate of secrecy that does limit the free flow of ideas and information that are vital for successful science. A desire by funders or research workers in the Science Base to obtain IPRs may also affect the direction of publicly funded

research, encouraging short-term, applied research that has merit but is usually better done in industry if a vibrant industrial base exists. The longer-term work on which industry relies may be displaced partially or reduced.... Patents can provide valuable, although sometimes expensive, protection for inventions. They therefore encourage invention and exploitation, but usually limit competition. They can make it impracticable for others to pursue scientific research within the areas claimed, and because inventions cannot be patented if they are already public knowledge, they can encourage a climate of secrecy. This is anathema to many scientists who feel that a free flow of ideas and information is vital for productive research. Additionally, research by others may be constrained by patents being granted that are inordinately broad in scope — a particular risk in the early stages of development of a field. This is bad for science and bad for society.' "Keeping Science Open: The Effects of Intellectual Property Policy on the Conduct of Science" (London: Royal Society, 2003).

8. <http://portal.unesco.org/shs/en/ev.php-URL_ID=1881&URL_DO=DO_TOPIC&URL SECTION=201.html> — the Declaration was adopted by UNESCO in 1997 and endorsed by the United Nations General Assembly in 1998.

9. Thanks to Alain Pottage for clarifying the issue at stake here.

10. For background information see <http://www.epo.org/aboutus/press/background-ers.html>; for the settlement see <http://www.epo.org/topics/news/2007/20071120a.html>.

11. An excellent discussion of the issues discussed in the following paragraphs can be found in S. A. Merrill and A.-M. Mazza et al., *Reaping the Benefits of Genomic and Proteomic Research: Intellectual Property Rights, Innovation, and Public Health* (Washington, D.C.: National Academies Press, 2006).

12. Thanks to Siva Thambisetty for this clarification.

13. This has been a key issue in debates over 'biopiracy' — as these mainly concern plant material, although sometimes with potential medical uses, I do not discuss these here.

14. Available at <http://www.nytimes.com/2006/05/05/business/ 05patent.html>.
15. I have simplified the issues for reasons of space — for a fuller discussion see Merrill and Mazza et al. (2006), p. 64.
16. Many of these issues are well discussed in contributions to a special issue of the journal *BioSocieties on Evidence Based Medicine and Randomised Control Trials*, see also A. Wahlberg and L. McGoey, "An Elusive Evidence Base: The Construction and Governance of Randomized Controlled Trials", *Biosocieties* 2, no. 1 (2007): 1–10.
17. See their 2004 'Conflict of Interest' Report, available at <www.nih.gov/ about /ethics_COI_panelreport.pdf>.
18. Mario Biagioli addresses some of these issues in his work on credit economies and scientific organization. M. Biagioli, "The Instability of Authorship: Credit and Responsibility in Contemporary Biomedicine", *Faseb Journal* 12, no. 1 (1998): 3–16. M. Biagioli, "Patent Republic: Representing Inventions, Constructing Rights and Authors", *Social Research* 73, no. 4 (2006): 1129–72.

References

Abraham, J. "Drug Trials and Evidence Bases in International Regulatory Context". *Biosocieties* 2, no. 1 (2007): 41–56.
Angell, M. *The Truth About the Drug Companies: How They Deceive Us and What to Do About It.* New York: Random House, 2004.
Association of University Technology Managers. *US University Activity Survey: FY 2006.* Association of University Technology Mangers, 2007.
Biagioli, M. "The Instability of Authorship: Credit and Responsibility in Contemporary Biomedicine". *Faseb Journal* 12, no. 1 (1998): 3–16.
———. "Patent Republic: Representing Inventions, Constructing Rights and Authors". *Social Research* 73, no. 4 (2006): 1129–72.
Boyle, J. "Enclosing the Genome: What Squabbles over Genetic Patents could teach us". *Persectives on Properties of the Human Genome Projects* 50 (2003): 97–122.

Davies, S.M. "Pharmacogenetics, Pharmacogenomics and Personalized Medicine: Are We There Yet?" *Hematology* 1 (2006): 111–17.

Davis, P.K. and J.J. Kelley et al. "ESTs Stumble at the Utility Threshold". *Nature Biotechnology* 23, no. 10 (2005): 1227–29.

Demaine, L.T. and A.X. Fellmeth. "Reinventing the Double Helix: A Novel and Non-Obvious Reconceptualization of the Biotechnology Patent". *Stanford Law Review* 55, no. 2 (2002): 303–462.

Elliot, C. "Pharma Buys A Conscience". *The American Prospect* 12, no. 7 (2001): 16–20.

———. "When Pharma goes to the Laundry: Public Relations and the Business of Medical Education". *Hastings Center Report* 34, no. 5 (2004): 18–23.

Ernst & Young. *Beyond Borders: Global Biotechnology Report 2007*. Ernst & Young, 2007.

Gold, E.R. *Body Parts: Property Rights and the Ownership of Human Biological Materials*. Washington, D.C.: Georgetown University Press, 1996.

Goldstein, D.B. and J.N. Hirschhorn. "In Genetic Control of Disease, Does 'Race' Matter?" *Nature Genetics* 36, no. 12 (2004): 1243–44.

Gottweis, H. and R. Triendl. "South Korean Policy Failure and the Hwang Debacle". *Nature Biotechnology* 24, no. 2 (2006): 141–43.

Healy, D. "Let Them Eat Prozac: The Unhealthy Relationship Between the Pharmaceutical Industry and Depression". New York: New York University Press, 2004.

Heath, D. and R. Rapp et al. "Genetic Citizenship". In *Companion to the Anthropology of Politics*, edited by D. Nugent and J. Vincent. Oxford: Blackwell Publishing, 2004.

Jordan, B. "Personal Genomics, for Fun or for Real?" *M S-Medecine Sciences* 24 (2008): 91–94.

Kass, L.R. "The Wisdom of Repugnance". *New Republic* 216, no. 22 (1997): 17–26.

Kay, L.E. "The Molecular Vision of Life: Caltech, the Rocketeller Foundation, and the Rise of the New Biology". New York and Oxford: Oxford University Press, 1993.

Kendall, T. and L. McGoey. "Truth, Disclosure and the Influence of Industry on the Development of NICE Guidelines: An Interview with Tim Kendall". *Biosocieties* 2, no. 1 (2007): 129–40.

Kennedy, D. "Enclosing the Research Commons". *Science* 294, no. 5550 (2001): 2249–.

Lander, E.S. and L.M. Linton et al. "Initial Sequencing and Analysis of the Human Genome". *Nature* 409, no. 6822 (2001): 860–921.

Latour, B. *Science in Action: How to Follow Scientists and Engineers Through.* Milton Keynes: Open University Press, 1987.

MacLeod, C. *Inventing the Industrial Revolution: The English Patent System, 1660–1800.* Cambridge: CUP, 1988.

McGuire, A.L. and T. Caulfield et al. "Science and Society: Research Ethics and the Challenge of Whole-Genome Sequencing". *Nature Reviews Genetics* 9 (2008): 152–56.

McGuire, A.L. and M.K. Cho et al. "Medicine: The Future of Personal Genomics". *Science* 317, no. 5845 (2007): 1687–87.

Merrill, S.A. and A.-M Mazza et al. *Reaping the Benefits of Genomic and Proteomic Research: Intellectual Property Rights, Innovation, and Public Health.* Washington, D.C.: National Academies Press, 2006.

Moynihan, R. and A. Cassels. *Selling Sickness: How the World's Biggest Pharmaceutical Companies are Turning us all into Patients.* New York, N.Y.: Nation Books, 2005.

Novas, C. "The Political Economy of Hope: Patients' Organizations, Science and Biovalue". *Biosocieties* 1, no. 3 (2006): 289–305.

———. "What is the Bioscience Industry Doing to Address the Ethical Issues it Faces?" *Plos Medicine* 3, no. 5 (2006): 600–01.

Ong, A. "Ecologies of Expertise: Assembling Flows, Managing Citizenship". In *Global Assemblages: Technology, Politics and Ethics as Anthropological Problems*, edited by A. Ong and S.J. Collier. Oxford: Blackwell Publishing, 2005.

Parry, B. *Trading the Genome: Investigating the Commodification of Bio-Information.* New York, Chichester: Columbia University Press, 2004.

Pearson, T.A. and T.A. Manolio. "How to Interpret a Genome-Wide Association Study". *Jama-Journal of the American Medical Association* 299, no. 11 (2008): 1335–44.

Petryna, A. "Drug Development and the Ethics of the Globalized Clinical Trial". *School of Social Science* (New School for Social Research), Working Paper, October 2005.

———."Clinical Trials Offshored: On Private Sector Science and Public Health." *Biosocieties* 2, no. 1 (2007): 21–40

Petryna, A. and A. Lakoff et al., eds. *Global Pharmaceuticals: Ethics, Markets, Practices.* Durham, N.C.: Duke University Press, 2006.

Rapp, R. and K.S. Taussig et al. "Genealogical Disease: Where Hereditary Abnormality, Biomedical Explanation, and Family Responsibility Meet". In *Relative Matters: New Directions in Kinship Study*, edited by S. Franklin and S. McKinnon. Durham, N.C.: Duke University Press, 2002.

Ready, T. "Company Pushes Broad-Ranging Patent Claim". *Nat Med* 8, no. 10 (2002): 1048–48.

Relman, A.S. and M. Angell. "Americas' Other Drug Problem". *New Republic* 227, no. 25 (2002): 27–41.

Rheinberger, H.-J. *Toward a History of Epistemic Things: Synthesizing Proteins in the Test Tube.* Stanford: Stanford University Press, 1997.

———. "Beyond Nature and Culture: Modes of Reasoning in the Age of Molecular Biology and Medicine". *Living and Working with the New Medical Technologies*, edited by M. Lock, Allan Young, and Alberto Cambrosio. Cambridge: Cambridge University Press, 2000.

Rose, N. "The Politics of Life Itself". *Theory, Culture & Society* 18, no. 6 (2001): 1–30.

———. *The Politics of Life Itself: Biomedicine, Power and Subjectivity in the Twenty First Century.* Princeton, NJ: Princeton University Press, 2006.

Royal Society of London. *Keeping Science Open: The Effects of Intellectual Property Policy on the Conduct of Science.* London: Royal Society, 2003.

Scheper-Hughes, N. "The Global Traffic in Human Organs". *Current Anthropology* 41, no. 2 (2000): 191–224.

Scheper Hughes, N. and L. Waquant, eds. *Commodifying Bodies.* London: Sage, 2002.

Scott, R. *The Body as Property.* London: Allen Lane, 1981.

Shapin, S. *A Social History of Truth: Civility and Science in Seventeenth-Century England.* Chicago, London: University of Chicago Press, 1994.

Smith, J.S. *Patenting the Sun: Polio and the Salk Vaccine.* New York: W. Morrow, 1990.

Tate, S.K. and D.B. Goldstein. "Will Tomorrow's Medicines Work for Everyone?" *Nature Genetics* 36, no. 11 (2004): S34–S42.

Taussig, K.S. and D. Heath et al. "Flexible Eugenics: Technologies of the Self in the Age of Genetics". In *Genetic Nature/Culture*, edited by A.H. Goodman, D. Heath, and M.S. Lindee. Berkeley: University of California Press, 2003.

Triggle, D.J. "Patenting the Sun: Enclosing the Scientific Commons and Transforming the University — Ethical Concerns". *Drug Development Research* 63, no. 3 (2004): 139–49.

Venter, J.C. and M.D. Adams et al. "The Sequence of the Human Genome". *Science* 291, no. 5507 (2001): 1304–51.

Wahlberg, A. and L. McGoey. "An Elusive Evidence Base: The Construction and Governance of Randomized Controlled Trials". *Biosocieties* 2, no. 1 (2007): 1–10.

Weber, M. *The Vocation Lectures.* Indianopolis, IN: Hackett Publishing Co., 2004.

Whittington, C.J. and T. Kendall et al. "Selective Serotonin Reuptake Inhibitors in Childhood Depression: Systematic Review of Published versus Unpublished Data". *Lancet* 363, no. 9418 (2004): 1341–45.

————. "Are the SSRIs and Atypical Antidepressants Safe and Effective for Children and Ddolescents?" *Current Opinion In Psychiatry* 18, no. 1 (2005): 21–25.

Chapter 6

A GLOBAL DEAL ON CLIMATE CHANGE

Nicholas Stern[1]

INTRODUCTION

Greenhouse gas (GHG) emissions are externalities in that they damage others but the cost is not borne by the emitter of pollution. Thus 'without policy' "the polluter does not pay" and therefore has no incentive to limit the damage inflicted on others. This represents the biggest market failure the world has seen. We all produce emissions, people around the world are already suffering from past emissions, and current emissions, if they are not curbed, will have potentially catastrophic impacts in the future. Thus these emissions are not ordinary, localised externalities such as congestion. Risk on a global scale is at the core of the issue. So too are ethics since first this is a highly inequitable process, the rich countries are responsible for most past emissions and poor countries are hit hardest, and second we have to think about relative valuation of costs and benefits far into the future. These basic features of the problem must shape the economic analysis we bring to bear; failure to do this will, and has, produced approaches to policy which are profoundly misleading and indeed dangerous.

In this chapter I will set out what I think is an appropriate way to examine the economics of climate change, given the unique scientific and economic challenges posed, and to suggest implications for emissions targets, policy instruments and global action. The subject is complex and very wide-ranging. It is a subject of vital importance but one in which the economics is fairly young. A central challenge is to provide the economic tools necessary as quickly as possible, because policy decisions are both urgent and moving quickly — particularly following the UNFCCC meetings in Bali in December 2007. The relevant decisions can be greatly improved if we bring the best economic analyses and judgements to the table in real time.

A brief description of the scientific processes linking climate change to GHG emissions will help us to understand how they should shape the economic analysis. First, people through their consumption and production decisions emit GHGs. Carbon dioxide is especially important, accounting for around three-quarters of the human-generated global warming effect; other relevant GHGs include methane, nitrous oxide and HFCs. Second, these flows accumulate into stocks of GHGs in the atmosphere. It is overall stocks of GHGs that matter and not their place of origin. The rate at which stock accumulation occurs depends on the 'carbon cycle', including the Earth's absorptive capabilities and other feedback effects. Third, the stock of GHGs in the atmosphere traps heat and results in global warming: how much depends on "climate sensitivity". Fourth, the process of global warming results in climate change. Fifth, climate change affects people, species and plants in a variety of complex ways, most notably via water in some shape or form: storms, floods, droughts, sea-level rise. These changes will potentially transform the physical and human geography of the planet, affecting where and how we live our lives. Each of these five links involves considerable uncertainty. The absorption-stock accumulation, climate-sensitivity, and warming-climate change links all involve time lags.

The key issues in terms of impacts are not simply or mainly about global warming as such — they concern climate change more broadly. Understanding these changes requires specific analysis of how climate will be affected regionally. Levels and variabilities of rainfall depend on the functioning of weather and climate for the world as a whole. As discussed below, temperature increases of 4–5°C on average for the world would involve radical and dangerous changes for the whole planet with widely differing, often extreme, local impacts. Further, the challenge, in large measure, is one of dealing with the consequences of *change* and not only of comparing long-run equilibria. Under business-as-usual (BAU), over the next two centuries we are likely to see change at a rate which is fast-forward in historical time and on a scale that the world has not seen for tens of millions of years.

This very brief and over-simplified description of the science carries key lessons for the economics. The scientific evidence on the potential risks is now overwhelming, as demonstrated in the recent IPCC Fourth Assessment Report or AR4 (IPCC 2007). I am not a climate scientist. As an economist, my task is to take the science, particularly its analysis of risks, and think about its implications for policy. Only by taking the extraordinary position that the scientific evidence shows that the risks are definitely negligible should economists advocate doing nothing now. The science clearly shows that the probability and frequency of floods, storms, droughts and so on, is likely to continue to grow with cumulative emissions, and that the magnitude of some of these impacts could be catastrophic.

Whilst an understanding of the greenhouse effect dates from the 19th century,[2] in the last decade, and particularly in the last few years, the science has fortunately started to give us greater guidance on some of the possible probability distributions linking emissions and stocks to possible warming and climate change, thus allowing us to bring to the table analytical tools on economic policy towards risk.

The brief description of the science above tells us that GHG emissions are an externality which is different from our usual examples in four key ways: (i) it is global in its origins and impacts; (ii) some of the effects are very long-term and governed by a flow-stock process; (iii) there is a great deal of uncertainty in most steps of the scientific chain; and (iv) the effects are potentially very large and many may be irreversible. Thus it follows that the economic analysis must place at its core: (a) the economics of risk and uncertainty; (b) the links between economics and ethics (there are major potential policy trade-offs both within and between generations), as well as notions of responsibilities and rights in relation to others and the environment; and (c) the role of international economic policy. Further, the potential magnitude of impacts means that for much of the analysis, we have to compare strategies which can have radically different development paths for the world. We cannot, therefore, rely only on the methods of marginal analysis. Here I attempt to sketch briefly an analysis which brings these three parts of economics to centre stage. It is rather surprising, indeed worrying, that much previous analysis of practical policy has relegated some or all of these three key pieces of economics to the sidelines.

THE STRUCTURE OF THE ARGUMENT

The structure of the argument on stabilization is crucial and we begin by setting that out before going into analytical detail. The choice of a stabilization target shapes much of the rest of policy analysis and discussion, because it carries strong implications for the permissible flow of emissions and thus for emissions reductions targets. The reduction targets, in turn, shape the pricing and technology policies.

Understanding the risks from different strategies is basic to an understanding of policy. Many articulated policies for risk reduction work in terms of targets, usually expressed in terms of emission flows, stabilization levels or average temperature increases. The last of these has the advantage that it is (apparently) easier for the general public to understand. The problem is that this apparent ease conceals crucial elements that matter greatly to social and economic outcomes — it is the effects on storms, floods, droughts and sea-level rise that are of particular importance, and a heavy focus on temperature can obscure this. Further, and crucially, temperature outcomes are highly stochastic and cannot be targeted directly. Emissions can be more easily controlled by policy. However, it is the stocks that shape the warming. Thus there are arguments for and against each of the three dimensions. We shall opt for stock targets, on the basis that they are closest to the phenomenon that drives climate change and the most easily expressed in one number.

An alternative focus for policy is the price of GHGs rather than quantities. In a perfectly understood non-stochastic world, standard duality theory says that price and quantity tools are essentially mirror images and can be used interchangeably. However, where risk and uncertainty are important and knowledge is highly imperfect we have to consider the relative merits of each. For the most part we ignore the difference between risk and uncertainty here (where the latter is used strictly in the Knightian sense of unknown probabilities), but it is a very important issue (Henry 2006; Stern 2007, pp. 38–39) and a key topic for further research.

We begin by setting out some of the major risks from climate change, and argue that these risks point to the need for both stock and flow targets, guided by an assessment of the costs involved in achieving them. Long-term stabilization (or stock) targets are associated with a range of potential flow paths, although the stock target exerts a very powerful influence on their shape. The choice of a particular flow path would be influenced by the expected pattern of costs over time. The target flow paths can then be associated with a path for marginal costs of abatement, if we think of efficient policy designed to keep flows to the levels on the path, in particular by using a price for carbon set at the marginal abatement cost (MAC). Essentially, the economics of risk points to the need for stock and flow quantity targets and the economics of costs and efficiency to a price mechanism to achieve the targets.

A policy which tries to start with a price for marginal GHG damages has two major problems: (i) the price estimate is highly sensitive to ethical and structural assumptions on the future; and (ii) there is a risk of major losses from higher stocks than anticipated, since the damages rise steeply with stocks and many are irreversible.

Formal modelling of damages can supplement the argument in three ways. First, it can provide indicative estimates of overall damages to guide strategic risk analysis. Second, it can provide estimates of marginal damage costs of GHGs, for comparison with MACs. Third, and most important in my view, it can help to clarify key trade-offs and the overall logic and key elements of an argument.

A useful analogy is the role of Computable General Equilibrium Models (CGMs) in discussions of trade policy. These have much more robust foundations than aggregative models on the economics of climate change yet their quantitative results are also very sensitive to assumptions and they also leave out so much that is important to policy. Thus most economists would not elevate them to the main plank of an argument on trade policy. That policy would usually be better founded on an understanding of economic theory and of economic history, together with country studies and particular studies of the context and issues in question.

However, as the Stern Review stressed, such analysis has very serious weaknesses and must not be taken too literally. It is generally forced to aggregate into a single good, and in so doing misses a great deal of the crucial detail of impacts — on different dimensions and in different locations — which should guide risk analysis. It is forced to make assumptions about rates and structures of growth over many centuries. Further, it will be sensitive to the specification of ethical frameworks and parameters. Thus its estimates of marginal social costs of damages provide a very weak foundation for policy. This type of modelling does have an important supplementary place in an analysis, but all too often it has been applied naively and transformed into the central plank of an argument.

Our analysis of risks and targets points to the need for aggregate GHG stabilization targets of below 550 parts per million (ppm) carbon dioxide equivalents (CO_2e), arguably substantially below. This corresponds to cuts in global emissions flows of at least 30 per cent, and probably around 50 per cent, by 2050. These cuts may seem large in the context of (we hope) a growing world economy, but are not ambitious in relation to the risks we run by exceeding 550ppm CO_2e. And, given the avoided risks, the costs of around 1 per cent of world GDP p.a. of achieving this stabilization should be regarded as relatively low. The carbon price required to achieve these reductions (up to, say, 2030) would be around or in excess of \$30 per tonne of CO_2.

This chapter incorporates many important elements of the Stern Review, published on the web in October/November 2006 (see <http://www.sternreview.org.uk>, including Postscript) and in book form (Stern 2007) a year ago, but goes beyond it in many important ways — in relation to subsequent policy discussions, new evidence and analysis, and discussions in the economics literature.

There are three further parts to this chapter. The second part focuses on risks and how to reduce them, and on costs of abatement. The third part examines policy, and in particular the role of different policy instruments. The fourth and final part outlines what I see as the central elements of a global deal or framework for collaborative policy and discusses how that deal can be built and sustained.

STABILIZATION OF STOCKS OF GREENHOUSE GASES I: RISKS AND COSTS

Risks and Targets

The relation between the stock of GHGs in the atmosphere and the resulting temperature increase is at the heart of any risk analysis. The preceding link in the chain, the way the carbon cycle governs the process relating emissions to changes in stocks, and the subsequent link, from global average temperature to regional and local climate change, are full of risk as well. But the stock-temperature relationship is the clearest way to begin as it anchors everything else. Broadly conceived it is about 'climate sensitivity' — in terms of modelling, this is indicated by the expected eventual temperature increase from a doubling of GHG stocks.[3]

There are now a number of general circulation models (GCMs — also known as global climate models) that have been built to describe the links from emissions to climate change. The large ones work with a very large number of geographic cells, consume computer time extremely heavily and can be run only on some of the world's biggest computers. Nevertheless, particularly if combined with appropriate linking to a large number of other machines, they can be run many times for different possible parameter choices. Such exercises yield Monte Carlo estimates of probability distributions of outcomes. A discussion of various methods and models may be found in Meinshausen (2006) and in Chapter 1 of the Stern Review.

Table 6.1 is drawn from the models of the U.K.'s Hadley Centre. The work of the Hadley Centre was a particular focus of models for the Stern Review for a number of reasons. First, it is one of the world's finest climate science groups, with a very large computing capacity. Second, it was close by and the staffs were extremely accessible and helpful. Third, its probability distributions are fairly cautious, balanced and 'middle of the road' (Meinshausen 2006); this judgement is sustained by a comparison of their results with the subsequently published AR4 (IPCC 2007).

Table 6.1 presents estimated probabilities for eventual temperature increases (which take time to be established) relative to pre-industrial times (around 1850), were the world to stabilize at the given concentration of GHGs in the atmosphere measured in ppm CO_2e.

Concentrations are currently around 430ppm CO_2e (Stern Review, Figure 6.1 (Stern 2007, p. 5) — Kyoto GHGs), and are rising at around 2.5ppm CO_2e p.a. This rate appears to be accelerating, particularly as a result of the very rapid growth of emissions in China. On fairly conservative estimates (IEA 2007), China's energy-related emissions are likely to double by 2030, taking overall emissions from 6–7 to 12–15 gigatonnes (Gt).

TABLE 6.1
Likelihood (in %) of Exceeding a Temperature Increase at Equilibrium

Stabilization Level (in ppm CO_2e)	2°C	3°C	4°C	5°C	6°C	7°C
450	78	18	3	1	0	0
500	96	44	11	3	1	0
550	99	69	24	7	2	1
650	100	94	58	24	9	4
750	100	99	82	47	22	9

Source: Stern Review Box 8.1 (Stern 2007, p. 220) with some added information.

There seems little doubt that, under BAU, the annual increments to stocks would average somewhere well above 3ppm CO_2e, perhaps 4 or more, over the next century. That is likely to take us to around or well beyond 750ppm CO_2e by the end of the century. If we manage to stabilise there, that would give us around a 50–50 chance of a stabilization temperature increase above 5°C. This is a high probability of a disastrous transformation of the planet (see below).[4] The issue is still more worrying than that of dealing with very large damages with very low probability.

Further, we should emphasize that key positive feedbacks from the carbon cycle — such as release of methane from the permafrost, the collapse of the Amazon and thus the destruction of a key carbon sink, and reduction in the absorptive capacity of the oceans — have been omitted from the projected concentration increases quoted here. It is possible that stocks could become even harder to stabilize than this description suggests.

We do not really know what the world would look like at 5°C above pre-industrial times. The most recent warm period was around 3 million years ago when the world experienced temperatures 2–3°C higher than today (Jansen et al. 2007, p. 440). Humans (dating from around 100,000 years or so) have not experienced anything that high. Around 10,000–12,000 years ago, temperatures were around 5°C lower than today, and ice sheets came down to latitudes just north of London and just south of New York. As the ice melted and sea levels rose, England separated from the continent, re-routing much of the river flow. These magnitudes of temperature changes transform the planet.

At an increase of 5°C most of the world's ice and snow would disappear, including major ice sheets and, probably, the snows and glaciers of the Himalayas. This would eventually lead to sea-level rises of 10 metres or more, and would thoroughly disrupt the flows of the major rivers from the Himalayas, which serve countries comprising around half of the world's population. There would be severe torrents in the rainy season and dry rivers in the dry season. The world would probably lose more than half its species. Storms, floods and droughts would probably be much more intense than they are today.

Further tipping points could be passed, which together with accentuated positive feedbacks could lead to 'runaway' further temperature increase. The last time temperature was in the region of 5°C above pre-industrial times was in the Eocene period around 35–55 million years ago. Swampy forests covered much of the world and there were alligators near the North Pole. Such changes would fundamentally alter where and how different species, including humans, could live. Human life would probably become difficult or impossible in many regions that are currently heavily populated, thus necessitating large population movements, possibly or probably on a huge scale. History tells us that large movements of population often bring major conflict. And many of the changes would take place over 100–200 years rather than thousands or millions of years.

Whilst there is no way that we can be precise about the magnitude of the effects associated with temperature increases of this size, it does seem reasonable to suppose that they would, in all likelihood, be disastrous. We cannot obtain plausible predictions by extrapolating from 'cross-sectional' (Mendelsohn et al. 2000, p. 557) comparisons of regions with current temperature differences of around 5°C — comparisons between, say, Massachusetts and Florida miss the point. Nor, given the non-linearities involved, can we extrapolate from lower temperature increases (say 2°C) concerning which there is more evidence. Most people contemplating 5°C increases and upwards would surely attach a very substantial weight on keeping the probability of such outcomes down.

From this perspective, an examination of Table 6.1 suggests that 550ppm CO_2e is an upper limit to the stabilization levels that should be contemplated. 550ppm CO_2e is nevertheless rather dangerous, with a 7 per cent probability of being above 5°C and a 24 per cent probability of being above 4°C. The move to 650ppm CO_2e gives a leap in probability of being above 4°C to 58 per cent, and of being above 5°C to 24 per cent. Further, we should remember that the Hadley Centre probabilities are moderately conservative — one highly computationally intensive Monte Carlo estimate of climate sensitivity found a 4.2 per cent probability of temperatures exceeding 8°C (Stainforth et al. 2005). A concentration in the region of 550ppm CO_2e is clearly itself a fairly dangerous place to be and the danger posed by even higher concentrations looks unambiguously unacceptable. For this reason I find it remarkable that some economists continue to argue that stabilization levels around 650ppm CO_2e or even higher are preferable to 550ppm, or even optimal (Nordhaus 2007a, p. 166; Mendelsohn 2007, p. 95). It is important to be clear that the "climate policy ramp" (Nordhaus 2007b,

p. 687) advocated by some economists involves a real possibility of devastating climatic changes.

In thinking about targets for stabilization, we have to think about more than the eventual stocks. We must also consider where we start; costs of stabilization; and possibilities of reversal, or backing out, if we subsequently find ourselves in or approaching very dangerous territory. The costs of stabilization depend strongly on where we start. Starting at 430ppm CO_2e, stabilizing at 550ppm CO_2e or below would likely cost around 1 per cent of world GDP with good policy and timely decision-making; for stabilization at 450ppm CO_2e, it might cost 3 or 4 times as much (possibly more). With bad policy, costs could be still higher. Note that the comparison of costs between 450ppm and 550ppm CO_2e illustrates the cost of delay[5] — waiting for 30 years before strong action would take us to around 530ppm CO_2e, from which point the cost of stabilizing at 550ppm CO_2e would likely be similar to stabilizing at 450ppm CO_2e starting from now. Under most reasonable assumptions on growth and discounting, a flow of 1 per cent of GDP for 50–100 years starting now would be much less costly than a flow for a similar period of 4 per cent or so of GDP, starting 30 years later.

The above is basically the risk-management economics of climate change. For an expenditure of around 1 per cent (between –1 per cent and 3 per cent) of world GDP, we could keep concentration levels well below 550ppm CO_2e and ideally below 500ppm CO_2e. Whilst leaving the world vulnerable, this would avoid the reckless risks implied by the higher stabilisation concentrations (e.g. 650ppm CO_2e) advocated by some economists. Thinking about the information basis for this argument also points to caution. If (as is unlikely) the risks of high concentrations turn out to be low and we have taken action, we would still have purchased a cleaner, more bio-diverse and more attractive world, at modest cost. If our actions are weak and the central scientific estimates are correct, we will be in very dangerous circumstances from which it may be impossible or very costly to recover.

Costs of Abatement and Prices of GHGs

To this point our discussion of targets has focused on those for the stabilization of stocks. We must now ask about implications for emissions paths and how much, with good policy, they would cost. We have already anticipated part of the broad answer — around 1 per cent of world GDP p.a. to get below 550ppm CO_2e — but we must look at the argument in a little more detail.

Figure 6.1 illustrates possible paths for stabilization at 550ppm CO_2e (long-dashed), 500ppm CO_2e (dotted) and 450ppm CO_2e (dot-dashed); the solid line is BAU. There are many paths for stabilization at a given level — see, for example, Stern Review

FIGURE 6.1
BAU and Stabilization Trajectories for 450–550ppm CO_2e

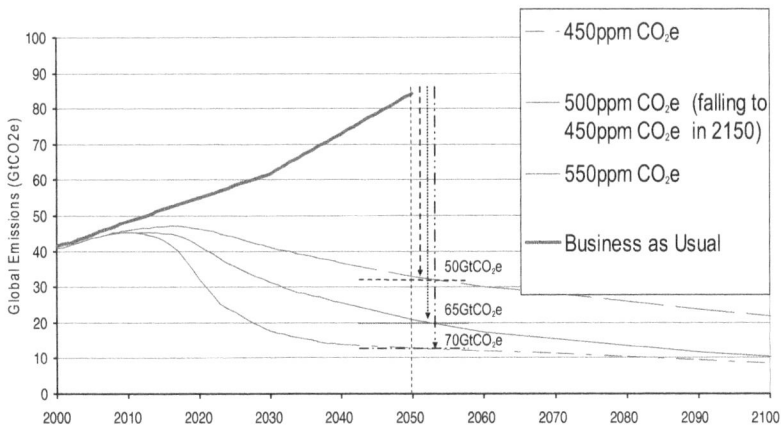

Source: Stern Review, Figure 8.4 (Stern 2007, p. 233).

Figure 8.2 (Stern 2007, p. 226) — but all of them are a similar shape to those shown (if a path peaks later it has to fall faster). And if the carbon cycle weakens, the cuts would have to be larger to achieve stabilization at a given level — see Stern Review Figure 8.1 (Stern 2007, p. 222). Broadly speaking, however, a path stabilizing at 550ppm CO_2e or below will have to show emissions peaking in the next 20 years. For lower stabilization levels, the peak will have to be sooner. The magnitudes of the implied reductions between 2000 and 2050 are around 30 per cent for 550ppm CO_2e, 50 per cent for 500ppm CO_2e, and 70 per cent for 450ppm CO_2e. Cuts relative to BAU are indicated in the figure.

Figure 6.2 shows that, to achieve these cuts in emissions, it will be necessary to take action across the board and not in just 2 or 3 sectors such as power and transport. For the world as a whole, energy emissions represent around two-thirds of the total and non-energy around one-third. Land use change, mainly deforestation and degradation of forests, accounts for nearly 20 per cent of the total. Given that the world economy is likely to be perhaps 3 times bigger in mid-century than it is now; absolute cuts of around 50 per cent would require cuts of 80–85 per cent in emissions per unit of output. Further, since emissions from some sectors (in particular agriculture) will be difficult to cut back to anything like this extent, and since richer countries should make much bigger proportional reductions than poor countries (see Section 4), richer countries will need to have close to zero emissions in power (electricity) and transport by 2050. Close-to-zero emissions in power are indeed possible and this would enable close-to-zero emissions for much of transport. This would, however, require radical changes to the source and use of energy, including much greater energy efficiency. Achieving the necessary reductions would also require an end to deforestation. However, the totality of such reductions would not result in a

FIGURE 6.2
Reducing Emissions Requires Action Across Many Sectors

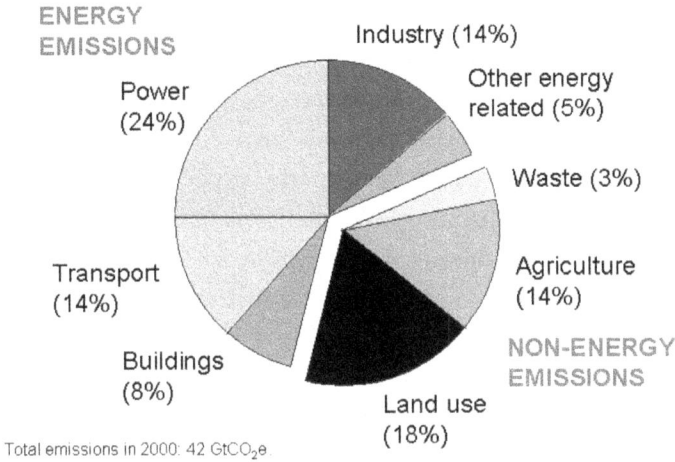

ENERGY
EMISSIONS

Industry (14%)

Power
(24%)

Other energy
related (5%)

Waste (3%)

Transport
(14%)

Agriculture
(14%)

NON-ENERGY
EMISSIONS

Buildings
(8%)

Land use
(18%)

Total emissions in 2000: 42 GtCO$_2$e.

Source: Stern 2007, p. 196.

radical change in way of life to the extent of that brought by electricity, rail, automobiles or the Internet.

On the path for stabilization there would be different options for cutting emissions that would be more prominent at different times. In the earlier periods there would be greater scope for energy efficiency and halting deforestation, and with technical progress there will be, and are already, strong roles for different technologies in power and transport.

It is very important to recognize that costs of 1 per cent of GDP do not necessarily slow medium- or long-term growth rates. They are like a one-off 1 per cent increase in prices from 'doing energy' in different ways. Further, there is a real possibility that incentives to discovery could generate a Schumpeterian burst of growth — on such possibilities see recent work by Aghion (2007). The scale of markets for new technologies will be very large (IEA

2006); see also Fankhauser et al. (2007) for an assessment of investment and employment opportunities, which are likely to be positive.[6]

Finally, reducing GHGs can bring strong benefits elsewhere. Cleaner energy can provide greater energy security and energy access. It can give reductions in local air pollution. Cleaner transport policies can increase life expectancy. Combating deforestation can protect watersheds, sustain biodiversity and promote local livelihoods. Taking these associated benefits into account would reduce cost estimates further.

In summary, looking back after a year, we would suggest that subsequent evidence and analysis have confirmed the range of our cost estimates for stabilization, or indicated that they may be on the high side. Good policy and timely decision-making are, however, crucial to keeping costs down. And we would emphasize that taking a clear view now of a stabilization goal allows for a measured and careful adjustment allowing for the replacement cycles of capital goods. Waiting-and-seeing, or a "climate policy ramp", risks not only excessive and dangerous levels of stocks but also much more costly abatement if, as is likely, there is a subsequent realization that the response has been delayed and inadequate.

POLICY INSTRUMENTS

At the heart of good policy will be a price for GHGs — this is a classic and sound approach to externalities and is crucial for an incentive structure both to reduce GHG emissions and to keep costs of abatement down. Indeed, in a world without any other imperfections it would be a sufficient instrument for optimal policy. But it will not be enough in our world given the risks, urgency, inertia in decision-making, difficulty of providing clear and credible future price signals in an international framework, market imperfections, unrepresented consumers, and serious concerns about equity. A second plank of policy will have to embrace technology and accelerate its development. Third, policy should take account of information and transactions costs, particularly in relation to energy efficiency. Fourth, it should provide an international framework to help with combating deforestation which is subject to a number of market failures. And fifth, policy should have a strong international focus, to promote collaboration, take account of equity, and reduce global costs.

Careful analytical investigation by economists of policies on climate change involves the whole range of the tools of our trade, including the economics of risk and uncertainty, innovation and technology, development and growth, international trade and investment, financial markets, legal issues, ethics and welfare as well as the whole range of public and environmental economics. It will no doubt require the development of further analytical methods. And it necessitates close collaboration with scientists and other social scientists.

Our focus here in this very brief discussion of policy will be on price-oriented mechanisms and on technology, but we should also note a sixth key element that is often overlooked in discussions of economic policy, namely how preferences change as a result of public discussion. This was an integral part of John Stuart Mill's (Mill 1972 [1861], p. 262) perception of democracy and policy formation (see also the discussion in Chapter 9 of Stern et al. 2005). In this context, it involves a change in public understanding of responsible behaviour. Thus people will spend time on separating out different elements of waste for recycling, or they will drive more carefully, not only because there may be a financial incentive for recycling or penalties for bad driving, but also because they have a view of responsible behaviour.

Pricing an externality can be done in a number of ways. First, there is carbon taxation; second, carbon trading on the basis of trade in rights to emit which are allocated or auctioned; and third, implicit pricing via regulations and standards which insist on constraints on actions or technologies which involve extra cost but which imply reductions in emissions. Each of the three has different advantages and disadvantages and all three are likely to be used. Understanding the pros and cons, where the different mechanisms can and should be used, and how to deal with problems of overlaps, are all very important issues. We have the space to look briefly only at a few of the relevant considerations.

Taxes have the advantage of being implementable by individual governments without international agreement. All taxes are contentious but those on recognised 'bads' such as tobacco, alcohol or carbon emissions may be less so than others and allow the balance of taxes to adjust away from other taxes such as income or VAT; alternative uses of revenue are possible too, including those related to climate change. We should beware, though, of arguments about double dividends: environmental taxes have dead-weight losses in addition to their beneficial effects in addressing externalities. Taxes on GHGs would require measurement of GHGs, just as in trading, but taxes on petroleum products, coal or other fossil fuels can act as fairly good approximations, avoiding direct emission measurement, which can be relatively costly to small enterprises.

As discussed previously, where the world is perfect other than in relation to the tax in question, quantity controls and price measurements can have dual and essentially identical effects. Where there is risk, uncertainty and imperfections in this market and in other parts of the economy, there will be price uncertainty, quantity uncertainty, or both, depending on the policies chosen and the nature of the uncertainty. Both price certainty and quantity certainty are important: firms would like clear and simple price signals for decision-making; quantity overshooting on emissions is dangerous. With learning and readjustment of policy (although not so frequently as to confuse structures and issues) the difference in effects between a tax-orientated policy and a quantity/carbon-trading policy may not be so large. Given where we start, however, in my view the danger of overshooting emissions targets is of great significance.

Tradable quotas, the second method of establishing a price for GHGs, have the advantage of providing greater certainty about quantities of emissions than taxes. The European Union Emissions Trading Scheme (EUETS) has shown that a big part of the economy can be covered (currently around one half of European emissions) with relatively low administrative burdens by focusing on major emitting industries, such as power.

By starting with allocations which are not paid for, and moving to auctions, trading can build acceptance by industry because it allows for a less dramatic adjustment. Free allocation based on historical emissions do have important problems, however: they are likely to slow adjustment since immediate profit pressures are less; they can give competitive advantages to incumbent firms who may succeed in getting large quota allocations, thus reducing competition and promoting rent-seeking; and they forego public revenue. Thus moving to auctioning over time has strong advantages and should be a clear and transparent policy.

An aspect of quotas and trading that is crucial is their potential role in international efficiency and collaboration. Developing countries (see next section) have a strong and understandable sense of injustice. They see rich countries having first relied on fossil fuels for their development, and thus being largely responsible for the existing stocks of GHGs, then telling them to find another, and possibly more costly, route to development. They feel least responsible for the position we are in, yet they will be hit earliest and hardest.

International trading both provides for lower costs, from the usual arguments about international trade, and provides an incentive for poor countries to participate. These arguments on cost and collaboration are central to my view that there should be a very substantial focus on carbon trading in the policy of rich countries, with openness to international trade, backed by strong rich country targets for reductions, in order to maintain prices at levels which will give incentives both for reduction at home and purchase abroad. Rich and poor country targets will be discussed in the next section.

Price volatility is sometimes said to be a problem with quotas and trading and the EUETS is sometimes cited as an example. But that scheme provided some basic simple lessons which have been learnt: in its first stage (2005–07), giving away too many quotas collapsed the price. Quotas have been allocated with greater rigour and stringency in the second phase (2008–12) and the price for that phase is currently above €20 per tonne, already approaching the type of range indicated as necessary. Volatility can be reduced by (i) clarity, (ii) firmness of quotas, and (iii) broader and deeper markets — greater trading across sectors, periods, and countries. Particular measures for dealing with volatility should be analysed in relation to, or after, these broader more market-friendly approaches. And care should be taken not to restrict international trade as a result; for example, differences in caps on prices in different regions might, because of attempts to arbitrage where prices are different but fixed, make open trade difficult or impossible.

Further, difficulties arise in trading with countries which are not taking strong measures, price-based or otherwise, against climate change. There is, in principle, a case for levying appropriate border taxes on goods from countries which do not otherwise embody a carbon price. A system analogous to the operation of the border procedures for VAT could be envisaged. My own view is that this should be a last resort. There are many searching for arguments on protection that might climb on the bandwagon. The best way forward is to build international collaboration with a positive and constructive approach.

Regulation and standards can give greater certainty to industry. This can accelerate responses and allow the exploitation of economies of scale: lead-free petrol and catalytic converters are probably good examples. Misguided regulation, on the other hand, could reduce emissions in very costly ways. Again urgency points to a role for regulation/standards, and careful economic analysis can keep costs down. In thinking about these costs, however, we should remark that there are a number of examples in the history of the motor industry where innovations on safety or pollution were resisted by industry on cost grounds, only for compliance costs to turn out to be much lower than manufacturer predictions; for EPA vehicle emission control programmes, industry stakeholders predicted price changes to consumers that exceeded actual changes by ratios ranging from 2:1 to 6:1 (Anderson and Sherwood 2002).

Whilst all three of taxation, trading and regulation will have roles to play, it is important to think carefully about how they might interact. For example, if taxation and carbon trading overlap, there are likely to be problems in establishing a clear and uniform price for carbon, leading to confused signals and inefficiency. And strong regulatory targets such as renewables percentages could, without care, result in low demand on carbon markets. Figure 6.3 indicates how an appropriate carbon price can make renewables (here wind), CCS for coal, and

FIGURE 6.3
Levelized Costs of Different Technologies (£/MWh):
Carbon Price €40 per tonne CO_2

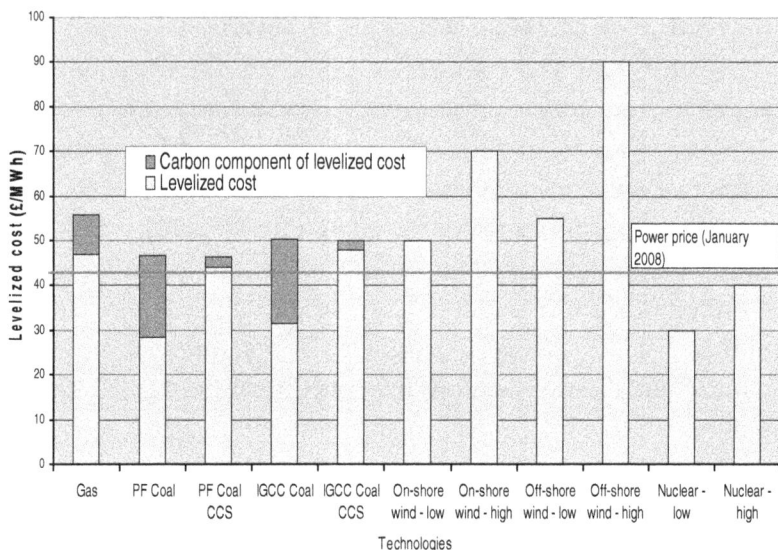

Note: PF – pulverised fuel
Source: BERR Energy Review 2006 (Fossil fuel price assumption (high gas price – Oil @ $70/bbl)).

nuclear competitive with standard techniques for electricity generation.

Our discussion of technology will be very brief, but in my view policy here will be of great importance — we cannot simply leave the correction of externalities to carbon markets or taxation. There is a standard argument on knowledge and technology which sees ideas and experience as having positive externalities. Figure 6.4 shows that experience is indeed important in the electricity industry — it seems that in a number of 'less mature' technologies costs can fall quite sharply with cumulative experience. Further, the rate of fall is different for different

FIGURE 6.4
Cost of Electricity for Different Technologies

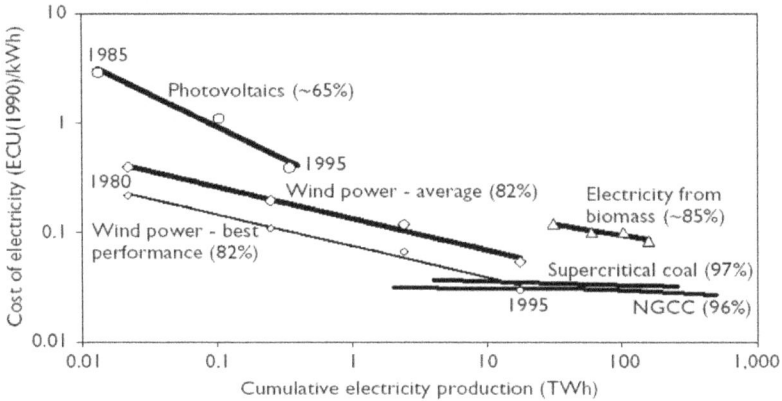

Source: Stern 2007, p. 254.

technologies. This tells us that public support for deployment — such as feed-in tariffs, which may be different for different technologies — has strong foundation. Care with applying such incentives is necessary to avoid the dangers of bureaucrats trying to pick private sector technological 'winners'.

Research and development (R&D) in basic technologies also require public support. It is remarkable how much public support for R&D in energy has fallen since the early 1980s — see Figure 6.5. Part of this was probably due to low energy prices,[7] but nevertheless the now-recognized urgency of developing low carbon technologies requires a strong reversal of this trend. Private and public sector R&D on energy have moved closely together and this is an area where public-private partnership to enhance both private and social returns, and to cover different risks, will be crucial. Fortunately the last few years have seen a number of exciting and promising developments, such as in materials and technologies, other than silicon, for photovoltaics.

FIGURE 6.5
Public Energy R&D Investments as a Share of GDP

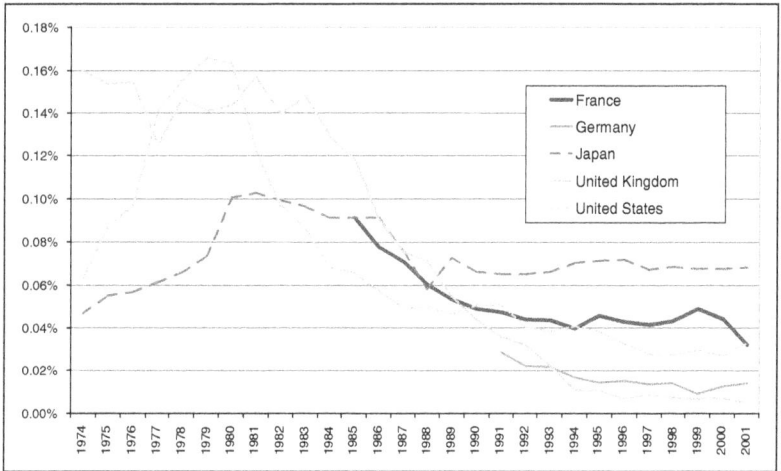

Source: Stern 2007, p. 401.

The international aspects of technology are crucial too. We all gain from reduced emissions if others adopt cleaner technologies quickly. Thus a balance of private returns to innovation, for example through patents, and rapid sharing must be found. This should be part of a global deal or framework to which we now turn.

A GLOBAL DEAL

Climate change is global in its origins and in its impacts. An effective response must therefore be organized globally and must involve international understanding and collaboration. Collaboration, if it is to be established and sustained, must be underpinned by a shared appreciation that the methods adopted are: *effective* (on the scale required); *efficient* (they keep costs down); and *equitable* (responsibilities and costs are allocated in ways which take account of wealth, ability and historical responsibility). The incentive structures must be such that solutions are incentive-compatible. And country-by-country political support must be built, as this is what will sustain policies over time.

Public support for action will be founded not only on recognition of the magnitude of the problem, but also on the realization that it is possible to construct collaborative policies that are effective, efficient and equitable. It is a great responsibility of economists to help design those policies. And they must do so urgently — the international discussion is moving quickly and key decisions will be taken over the next few years.

The following is my own attempt to describe the outline of a possible global deal based on the preceding analysis and on my own intensive experience over the last two years of involvement in public discussion. They take account of the UNFCCC meetings at Bali in December 2007. Let us begin with overall reductions targets and the allocation of responsibilities across countries. Our earlier discussions of trading, technologies, and deforestation will then allow us to see quickly the broad structure of a global deal. Let us be clear at the outset that this should not be seen in the overly formal way of a WTO discussion, founded in legal structures, with compliance driven by sanctions, and where no one is bound until the full deal is agreed. This is much more a framework in which each country, or group of countries, can assess its own responsibilities and targets with some knowledge of where the rest of the world is going and how it can interact.

On targets — a key element of *effectiveness*, or action on an appropriate scale — we should be clear how far the international discussion has already moved. The G8-G5 summit chaired by Germany in Heiligendamm in June 2007 declared a world target of 50 per cent reductions by 2050. As sometimes happens in international communiqués not all details (such as base date and levels of agreement amongst attendees) were clear; but it was a significant marker nonetheless. And it is broadly consistent with the type of stabilization range, around 500ppm CO_2e for example, discussed in Section 2. In what follows, unless otherwise stated, emissions reductions will be measured from 1990, covering all GHGs (in the 6-gas Kyoto sense) and emissions sources. The Heiligendamm 50 per cent target is for the world as a whole and it is generally agreed (see below) that, in the spirit of the Kyoto language of 'common but differentiated treatment', the richer countries should take responsibility for reductions bigger than the average. In what follows we shall think of rich country reductions as including those that are discharged by purchases on international markets.

At Bali in December 2007, three countries, Costa Rica, New Zealand and Norway declared targets of 100 per cent reductions by 2050, i.e. 'going carbon-neutral'. The latter two are highly likely to need international purchases to get there. Note too that reductions of more than 100 per cent are possible — many in developing countries would regard targets for rich countries above 100 per cent as appropriate, given past history — and that such reductions that would almost inevitably involve international purchase.

California has a target of 80 per cent reductions by 2050. France has its 'Facteur Quatre': dividing by 4, or 75 per cent reductions, by 2050 (Stern 2007, p. 516). The U.K. has a 60 per cent target but the Prime Minister indicated in November 2007 that this could be raised to 80 per cent (Brown 2007). Australia, under the new government elected at the end of November 2007, has now signed Kyoto and has a target of 60 per cent (Rudd 2007); 80 per cent is under consideration after the Garnaut

Review was published in summer 2008. Senators John McCain and Barack Obama, the U.S. presidential candidates, have both declared in favour of strong action.

Targets for 2050 seem far away but the long lifetime of many investments means that early decisions are needed to reach them. Intermediate targets are also being set. At the European Spring Council 20–30 per cent targets were set for 2020; Germany has set 40 per cent targets by 2020. The European Council also set targets for renewables and CCS for 2020 and beyond, but it is the overall emissions targets, and their achievement, which are crucial. How they are achieved country-by-country will vary and must take account of economic as well as environmental, social and political considerations. At Bali, many were pressing for rich countries to accept 25–40 per cent cuts by 2020. That is indeed in the right range for rich country cuts of 80 per cent by 2050 and is now at least an initial 2020 benchmark. Overall, in discussions of global and rich country targets, ranges consistent with the criteria of effectiveness and equity are now the basic benchmarks and many key commitments have been made. Delivery on targets at reasonable cost — essentially *efficiency* — is, of course, crucial and a challenge. Policies that could support this constituted the subject of Section 4 and should be at the heart of a global deal.

Let us, first, investigate equity in a little more detail. The history of flows and their relation to future stabilization targets should, in my view, be central to a discussion of equity. All too often, equity is seen solely or largely in terms of the relative level of future flows (for example, per capita convergence by 2050). A few numbers and a little basic arithmetic will help to understand the issues. Currently global emission flows are around 40–45 Gt CO_2e. With a world population of around 6 billion that means average global per capita emissions are around 7 tonnes. Given that the world population in 2050 will be around 9 billion, in order to achieve 50 per cent reductions (i.e. an aggregate flow of around 20 Gt CO_2e) by then, per capita emissions will have to be 2–2.5 tonnes. And since around 8 billion of these people will be in currently poor countries, those countries will have to be in that range[8] even if emissions in currently rich countries were to fall to zero. It is clear from this basic arithmetic that any effective global deal must have the currently poor countries at its centre.

From the point of view of equity the numbers are stark. The currently rich countries are responsible for around 70 per cent of the existing stock, and are continuing to contribute substantially more to stock increases than developing countries. The United States, Canada and Australia each emit over 20 tonnes of CO_2e (i.e. from all GHGs) per capita, Europe and Japan over 10 tonnes, China more than 5 tonnes, India around 2 tonnes, and most of sub-Saharan Africa much less than 1 tonne. Recent per capita CO_2 emissions (i.e. omitting other GHGs) for some countries are illustrated in Figure 6.6.

In the lower part of this graph are three big, fast-growing developing countries. China is growing especially quickly. Even with fairly conservative estimates, it is likely that, under BAU, China will reach current European per capita emissions levels within 20–25 years. With its very large population, over this time China under BAU will emit cumulatively more than the USA and Europe combined over the last 100 years. That is one indication of the urgency of finding a global response quickly.

But let us keep focused on equity. With 80 per cent reductions by 2050 Europe and Japan would be around the required 2 tonnes global average level. An 80 per cent reduction by the USA, Australia and Canada by 2050 would leave them around 4 tonnes, twice the required average level. Thus a 50 per cent overall reduction and an 80 per cent rich country reduction

FIGURE 6.6
Per Capita CO_2 Emissions
(in tonnes)

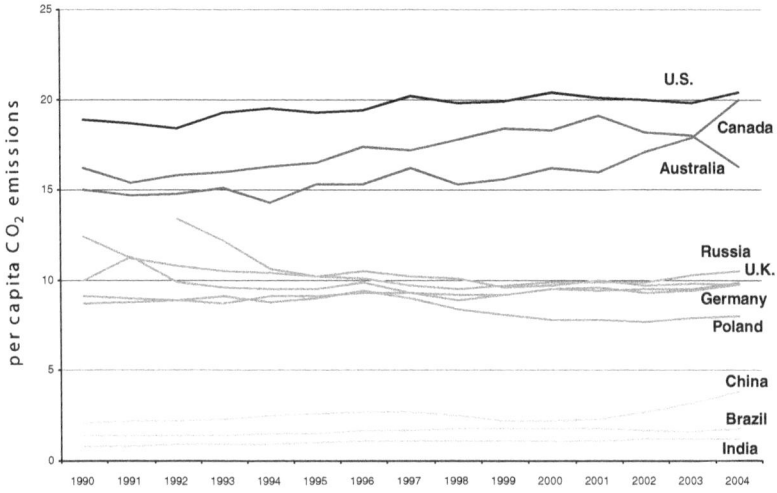

Source: CDIAC 2007.

would still leave average rich country flows above the world average in 2050.

Turning to stocks, let us think about the path from some initial level to a stock stabilization (to be specific suppose that level is 550ppm CO_2e), and about who consumes what along the way. We can think of the initial level as 280ppm CO_2e, corresponding to pre-industrial times (around 1850); or we could start 20 years ago (around 390ppm CO_2e), when the problems of climate change began to receive strong policy attention; or we could start now (around 430ppm CO_2e). One perspective on equity would be to see the difference between 280ppm CO_2e and 550ppm CO_2e as a reservoir sized 270ppm CO_2e which the world will get close to exhausting over the 200 years between 1850 and

2050. If we start the clock in the late 1980s or now, it would be a reservoir sized around 140ppm CO_2e or 120ppm CO_2e respectively.

From this perspective, equalizing the per capita flows of emissions — or the size of the glass drawn per person per year from the reservoir — by 2050, shortly before it is dry, is a very weak notion of equity. It takes no account of all the guzzling that took place by the better off over the preceding 50–200 years (depending on when we start the clock). There is a very big difference between a stock and a flow notion of equity. An 80 per cent reduction of flows by rich countries by 2050, in the context of a 50 per cent reduction overall, is not a target for which rich countries should congratulate themselves warmly as demonstrating a splendidly powerful commitment to equity. And the contract-and-converge argument for some common flow level, or for using such a level as the eventual basis of trading, on the asserted ground that there are 'equal rights to emit or pollute', does not seem to me to have special claim on our attention.[9] Rather the target of equalizing by 2050 (allowing for trade) may be seen as being a fairly pragmatic one, on which it might be possible to get agreement, and one which whilst only weakly equitable is a lot less inequitable than some other possibilities, such as less stringent targets for rich countries.

If we take any particular good it will generally be true that rich people consume more than poor people. That is simply an expression of their being richer. In the case of the reservoir, or the 'contents of the atmosphere', it is hard to think of an argument as to why rich people should have more of this shared resource than poor people. They are not exchanging their labour for somebody else's and they are not consuming the proceeds of their own land, or some natural resource which lies beneath it. I do not have any special 'correct' answer to the challenge of

understanding equity here, but it is a challenge we cannot avoid
discussing. Any global deal will have to involve some implicit or
explicit understanding over the sharing of this 'reservoir'.

The key elements of the global deal have, with one exception,
now been raised and discussed. Let me express the deal or
framework in terms of two groups of three headings, the first
covering targets and trade and the second covering programmes
for which public funding is likely to be required. This set of six
policies or programmes is the international part of a deal. The
domestic policies will vary across countries, using different
combinations of policy instruments and technologies as discussed
before. The six elements of a global deal are expressed in bullet
point form in Tables 6.2 and 6.3.

The first and second elements cover the overall targets and
trade both for rich and developing countries. The global target
was explained and justified in Section 2 and the distribution of
targets above in this section. The third, the importance of

TABLE 6.2
Key Elements of A Global Deal: Targets and Trade

Targets and Trade
- Confirm Heiligendamm **50%** cuts in world emissions by 2050 with rich country cuts at least **80%**
- Developing countries to take on **targets at latest by 2020** as rich countries demonstrate low-carbon growth, flows of funds, sharing technologies. Credible plans to reach 2 tonne/cap by 2050 — requires peaking before 2030
- Rich country reductions and trading schemes designed to be **open to trade with other countries**, including developing countries. **Supply side from developing countries** simplified to allow much bigger markets for emissions reductions: 'carbon flows' to rise to $50–$100bn p.a. by 2030

TABLE 6.3
Key Elements of A Global Deal: Funding

Funding Issues
• Strong initiatives, with public funding, on **deforestation** to prepare for inclusion in trading. For $10–15 bn p.a. could have a programme which might halve deforestation. Importance of global action and involvement of IFIs
• Demonstration and sharing of **technologies**: e.g. $5 bn p.a. commitment to feed-in tariffs for CCS coal would lead to 30+ new commercial size plants in the next 7–8 years
• Rich countries to deliver on Monterrey and Gleneagles commitments on **ODA** in context of extra costs of development arising from climate change: potential extra cost of development with climate change upwards of $80bn p.a.

emissions trading, was emphasised in Section 3. The justification for a major focus on GHG trading in policy lies in its promotion of both efficiency and collaboration. Unless financing flows for the extra costs of reducing emissions are available to poor countries, they are extremely unlikely to join the effort on the scale and pace required. They feel the inequities of the situation and phenomena acutely. Just when, they argue, they are beginning to overcome poverty, in part by rapid growth, they should not be asked to slow down. Financing, together with technology demonstration and transfer, will be needed to convince them that moving to a low-carbon growth path is not the same thing as moving to a low growth path. Hence, in the second element, it is important that there be a period of demonstration by the rich countries (2010–20) before developing countries make a final commitment. But peaking before

2030 and meeting the targets by 2050 would require designing and acting on plans now.

The third element refers to the short- and medium-term approaches to trading between rich and poor countries. The current system, the Clean Development Mechanism (CDM), was established by Kyoto and operates at the level of a project in a poor country (a so-called non-Annex 1 country in the Kyoto Protocol). If a firm in a rich country is part of a trading scheme (such as the EUETS) which recognizes the CDM then that firm can buy an emissions reduction achieved by the project, subject to the project using technologies or approaches from an admissible list. The amount of the notional reduction comes from comparing the project with a counterfactual — what the entity doing the project might otherwise have done. Approval of a project goes through the poor country authorities and a special institutional structure, currently in Bonn. The system is slow, cumbersome and very 'micro'.

Trading on the scale required to reach the type of targets discussed (see Table 6.2) requires a much simpler, 'wholesale' system.[10] At the same time, to get agreement with poor countries, it will have to continue to be 'one-sided', as in the CDM, i.e. you can gain from innovation, but are not penalized for BAU. Wholesale measures can include technological benchmarks such as employing CCS (currently excluded from CDM), or sectoral benchmarks such as getting below a certain amount of CO_2 per tonne of cement. As one-sided trading measures, the benchmarks could be set ambitiously.

After these trading mechanisms have been in place (with associated technology sharing) for a while, developing countries will be able to have confidence that a trading system can work on an appropriate scale. Then it would be reasonable to ask them to accept targets consistent with overall global goals in the context of a strong set of goals by rich countries. If we look for targets from poor countries now, the only ones that would be accepted would be far too loose and would knock the bottom out of international trading, i.e. collapse the price. And in the future these loose targets would be likely to form a baseline for subsequent discussion. That is why a staged approach is essential if currently poor countries are to accept participation in responsible global stabilization so that by 2050 their emissions average around 2 tonnes per capita. Recall that this is a half or a third of China's *current* level. It is very unlikely to be possible to find financial flows on the scale required to incentivise appropriate action from the public sector of rich countries. Witness the difficulty in getting resources for Overseas Development Assistance (ODA), which will be strained still further by the challenge of adaptation — see below. The trading system provides for private flows.

The public funding requirements are grouped under three heads in Table 6.3. Each of them would require a paper in itself for appropriate treatment and we can give only headlines. Deforestation accounts for up to 20 per cent of current emissions; the numbers are not easy to specify precisely — probably 5–8 Gt CO_2e p.a. These flows could be roughly halved in my view for around $5 per tonne of CO_2, taking into account opportunity costs of land and the institutional, administrative and enforcement measures necessary. Some have estimated higher costs (e.g. McKinsey — Enkvist et al. 2007) but there appear to be large amounts of 'initial' reductions available at lower costs, particularly if programmes are large-scale and coordinated across countries (for further discussion see Myers 2007; Nepstad et al. 2007; Anger and Sathaye 2007). This would help to avoid reduced deforestation in country A simply displacing activity and thus increasing deforestation in country B. Public sector flows can be combined with private sector flows as avoided deforestation is brought into the carbon trading process so that all countries are given incentives. Indeed one of the responsibilities of the publicly funded programme would be to work towards trading.

The second element in this second group, the demonstration and sharing of technologies, is urgent; financial resources must be made available and institutional arrangements designed. This is an important area for economic research. One problem of particular urgency, for reasons described above, is the demonstration of CCS for coal. There are no current plants using CCS for coal-fired generation on a commercial scale. From 2015 or 2020 the world will need most of its new coal-fired electricity generation plants to be operating with CCS if it is to have any chance of realising its targets. If CCS cannot work on the necessary scale, then we need to know soon and follow alternative strategies. However, at present it does look promising. There is geological work to be done to identify storage capacity, and careful legal and regulatory work to be done to allocate risk and responsibility. Geology and coal vary greatly across the world and many demonstrations of commercial-scale plants are necessary. Feed-in tariffs, worldwide, of around $5 billion p.a. could support 30+ such plants over the next 7–8 years and cover a broad range of examples.[11]

There should be support for many other technologies too. We do not know what the most efficient clean technologies will be in the future and the answers are likely to vary with location. CCS is emphasized here simply because we can be fairly confident that BAU will involve a great deal of coal for electricity over the next 20–30 years. Perhaps it will be a medium-term technology and be replaced by others over the longer term.

Finally, in the global deal, I would emphasise an element that has not been discussed here and which will be of great importance. Even with very responsible policies the world is likely to see an additional 1–2°C of warming over and above the 0.8°C it has already experienced. Adaptation will be necessary worldwide and particularly difficult for poor countries. Recently the UNDP has estimated additional costs for developing countries of around $85 billion p.a. by 2015 (UNDP 2007, p. 15). And it will presumably rise after that.

Such extra financing will be hard to find. It may be compared with the $150–200 billion p.a. extra that would arise if the OECD countries moved to 0.7 per cent GDP in ODA by 2015, as many of them have promised. The ODA promises of the 2002 UN Financing for Development conference in Monterrey; in connection with the Millennium Development Goals; and of the 2005 U.K.-chaired G8 Gleneagles summit on Africa, and preceding EU commitments in July, were powerfully argued and justified at the time. They took little account of climate change. If that aspect is added, as it should be given the magnitude of the challenge, and combined with the historical responsibilities for stocks of GHGs and the implied consequences for poor countries, then the argument for 0.7 per cent, in my view, becomes overwhelming. The Stern Review left the argument at that point, although a case could have been made for increasing the ODA targets.

The framework I have now described does, in my view, meet the criteria of: effectiveness — it is on the right scale; efficiency — it relies heavily on markets and market-orientated innovation; and equity — it does at least give some specificity to the "common but differentiated responsibility" already accepted internationally. It builds on existing commitments and some aspects of the current discussions in international fora. It is also designed to give some realistic opportunity for the major developing countries to become strongly involved, as they must if serious targets are to be agreed and achieved.

It is a framework which could allow all countries to move quickly along what they see to be a responsible path. What is very striking here is how broadly basic understandings have already been established. Country-by-country we see targets being erected and measures being set by individual countries recognizing their own responsibilities as they see international agreement being built. People seem to understand the arguments for action and collaboration on climate change much more readily than they do for international trade. But I do not want to pretend that the problems and necessary actions are universally recognized and accepted. Scientific agreement seems broad and deep but we cannot yet say that about economic policy and amongst economists. This is a time for exchange of ideas and intensive discussion. Economic policy is much too important here to be left to non-economists.

It is intensive public discussion that will, in my view be the ultimate enforcement mechanism. For example, in November 2007 we saw an Australian Prime Minister thrown out of office in part because of his perceived weakness on this issue. It is remarkable that when elections come around politicians recognize strong public interest and demand for action. And it has become a unifying and defining issue in the structures of Europe. It has not moved at the same pace in all countries but we are also seeing strong changes in perception in the key countries of the USA, China and India.

Beyond discussion there are some promising movements in world and individual country policy. Bali in December 2007 was a major step forward, with all countries involved broadly (but not universally) recognizing the need for overall 50 per cent cuts by 2050 and 25–40 per cent cuts by rich countries by 2020 (although only the phrase 'deep cuts' was agreed). There was progress on international action on deforestation. But it was the launch of negotiations only; it was not an agreement on a shared global framework.

The discussion of that global framework will move forward strongly over the next few years. The challenge is far-reaching, comprehensive and global, but it is manageable. The technological transformations and flows of funds required across countries and sectors will be large, the institutional and implementation challenges significant, but the costs of action are affordable and entirely consistent with sustainable growth and development. By contrast, the alternative of inaction or delay is not. The time to act is now.

It is vital that economics and economists are more strongly involved, particularly if the criteria of efficiency and equity are to play their proper role. It is the analytical application of these two criteria to practical policy problems that is at the heart of public economics. The challenge of climate change is especially difficult because it covers so much of the economy, is so long term, is so full of risk and uncertainty, is so demanding internationally, and is so urgent because of the problem itself and the pace of public discussion and decision-making. It is also a long-term problem, for analysis. We will be learning all the time and policy will be made and reformed over coming decades.

It is dangerous, in my view, for us as economists to seem to advocate weak policy and procrastination and delay under the banner of "more research to do" or "let's wait and see". The former argument is always true but we have the urgent challenge of giving good advice now, based on what we currently understand. And the latter in my view is misguided — waiting will take us into territory which we can now see is probably very dangerous and from which it will be very difficult to reverse. Acting now will give us, at fairly modest cost, a cleaner world and environment, even if, as seems very improbable, the vast majority of climate scientists have got it wrong. If we conclude that whatever the merits of the argument, it is all too difficult to make and implement policy, then we should at least be clear about the great magnitude of the risks of moving to concentrations of 650ppm CO_2e or more which are the likely consequences of no, weak, or delayed action.

It is hard to imagine a more important and fascinating problem for research. It will involve all our skills and more, and it will require collaboration across disciplines.

Notes

1. This chapter draws heavily and directly, omitting most of the technical economics, on the Richard Ely Lecture I gave to the American Economic Association Meeting in New Orleans in January 2008 which was published in the *American Economic Review* in May 2008.
2. Fourier recognized in the 1820s (Fourier 1827) that the atmosphere was trapping heat; three decades later, Tyndall (1861) identified the types of gases responsible for the trapping; and at the end of the century, Arrhenius (1896) gave calculations of the possible effects of doubling GHGs.
3. Climate modellers tend to define 'doubling' in relation to pre-industrial times. The relationship from stock to temperature increase is approximately logarithmic, so that doubling from other stock levels would be likely to yield a similar increase.
4. To avoid excessive length of discussion, we focus on 5°C, because it is an extremely dangerous increase and because its probability of occurrence under BAU is far from small. In a full analysis, one could and should look at the full range of possible concentrations and associated probability distributions for temperature increases.
5. There would be some negatives (more inflexible equipment in place) and some positives (more technical knowledge).
6. These assessments refer to the potential shifts of the demand side of labour markets — outcomes depend, of course on market structures.

7. Extensive privatization has probably played a role as well. For example, the U.K.'s nationalised National Coal Board and Central Electricity Generation Board had R&D departments of international distinction.

8. In this context I am referring to absolute emissions originating in the country rather than who pays.

9. Asserting equal rights to pollute or emit seems to me to have a very shady ethical grounding. Emissions deeply damage and sometimes kill others. Do we have a 'right' to do so?

10. This scale is derived from preliminary calculations using a trading model at the U.K. Department of Environment, Food and Rural Affairs (DEFRA).

11. Own calculations using, for example, the McKinsey cost curve, and working with power stations of a few hundred megawatts. I am grateful to Dennis Anderson for his advice.

References

Aghion, Philippe. "Environment and Endogenous Technical Change". Mimeographed. Harvard University, December 2007.

Anderson, J.F. and T. Sherwood. "Comparison of EPA and Other Estimates of Mobile Source Rule Costs to Actual Price Changes". SAE Technical Paper 2002-01-1980, Society of Automotive Engineers, Warrendale PA, 2002.

Anger, Niels and Jayant Sathaye. "Reducing Deforestation and Trading Emissions: Economic Implications for the post-Kyoto Carbon Market". Mimeographed. Centre for European Economic Research, 2007.

Arrhenius, Svante. "On the Influence of Carbonic Acid in the Air upon the Temperature of the Ground". *Philosophical Magazine* 41 (1896): 237–76.

Brown, Gordon. "Speech on Climate Change". Transcript of speech given to World Wildlife Fund, 19 November 2007, available at <http://www.pm.gov.uk/output/Page13791.asp> (accessed 2 January 2008).

CDIAC [Carbon Dioxide Information Analysis Center]. Website of the

Carbon Dioxide Information Analysis Center, United States Department of Energy, available at <http://cdiac.ornl.gov>, 2007.

Enkvist, Per-Anders, Tomas Naucler, and Jerker Rosander. "A Cost Curve for Greenhouse Gas Reduction". *The McKinsey Quarterly* 1 (2007): 35–45.

Fankhauser, Samuel, Friedel Sehlleier, and Nicholas Stern. "Climate Change, Innovation and Jobs". Mimeographed. IDEAcarbon, December 2007.

Fourier, Joseph. "Mémoire sur les Températures du Globe Terrestre et des Espaces Planétaires". *Mémoires de l'Académie Royale des Sciences* 7 (1827): 569–604.

Garnaut, Ross. "Will Climate Change Bring an End to the Platinum Age?". Paper presented at the inaugural S.T. Lee Lecture on Asia & The Pacific, Australian National University, Canberra, 29 November 2007.

Griscom Little, Amanda. "Clinton on the Record". *Grist*, 9 August 2007. Available from <http://www.grist.org/feature/2007/08/09/clinton/> (accessed 2 January 2007).

Hadley Centre. "Stabilising Climate to Avoid Dangerous Climate Change — A Summary of Relevant Research at the Hadley Centre". Available from <http://www.metoffice.com/research/hadleycentre/pubs/brochures> (accessed 9 November 2007).

Heal, Geoffrey. *Climate Change Economics: A Meta-Review and Some Suggestions*. Mimeographed. Columbia University, November 2007.

Henry, C. "Decision-Making Under Scientific, Political and Economic Uncertainty". Cahier no. DDX-06-12, Chaire Développement Durable, Laboratoire d'Econométrie de l'Ecole Polytechnique, Paris, 2006.

IEA [International Energy Agency]. *World Energy Outlook 2006*. International Energy Agency, Paris, 2006.

———. *World Energy Outlook 2007*. International Energy Agency, Paris, 2007.

IPCC [Intergovernmental Panel on Climate Change]. *Climate Change 2007: The Physical Science Basis: Contribution of Working Group I to the*

Fourth Assessment Report of the Intergovernmental Panel on Climate Change, edited by S. Solomon, D. Qin, M. Manning, Z. Chen, M. Marquis, K.B. Averyt, M. Tignor, and H.L. Miller. Cambridge: Cambridge University Press, 2007.

Jansen, E., J. Overpeck, K.R. Briffa, J.-C. Duplessy, F. Joos, V. Masson-Delmotte, D. Olago, B. Otto-Bliesner, W.R. Peltier, S. Rahmstorf, R. Ramesh, D. Raynaud, D. Rind, O. Solomina, R. Villalba, and D. Zhang. "Chapter 6: Palaeoclimate". In IPCC [Intergovernmental Panel on Climate Change], *Climate Change 2007: The Physical Science Basis: Contribution of Working Group I to the Fourth Assessment Report of the Intergovernmental Panel on Climate Change*, edited by S. Solomon, D. Qin, M. Manning, Z. Chen, M. Marquis, K.B. Averyt, M. Tignor, and H.L. Miller. Cambridge: Cambridge University Press, 2007.

Meinshausen, M. "What does a 2°C target mean for greenhouse Gas Concentrations? A brief analysis based on multi-gas emission pathways and several climate sensitivity uncertainty estimates". In *Avoiding Dangerous Climate Change*, edited by J.S. Schellnhuber, W. Cramer, N. Nakicenovic, T.M.L. Wigley, and G. Yohe. Cambridge: Cambridge University Press, 2006.

Mendelsohn, R.O., W.N. Morrison, M.E. Schlesinger, and N.G. Andronova. "Country-specific Market Impacts of Climate Change". *Climatic Change* 45, no. 3/4 (2000): 553–69.

Mendelsohn, Robert. Paper to Yale Symposium on the Stern Review, Yale Center for the Study of Globalization, February 2007, available from <http://www.ycsg.yale.edu/climate/forms/chapter8.pdf> (accessed 1 December 2007).

Mill, John Stuart. "Considerations of Representative Government". In *J.S. Mill: Utilitarianism, On Liberty and Considerations on Representative Government*, edited by H.B. Acton. London: J.M. Dent & Sons, 1972 [1861].

Myers, Erin C. "Policies to Reduce Emissions from Deforestation and Degradation (REDD) in Tropical Forests: An examination of the issues facing the incorporation of REDD into market-based climate policies". Resources for the Future Discussion Paper 07-50. Washington, D.C.: Resources for the Future, December 2007.

Nepstad, Daniel, Britaldo Soares-Filho, Frank Merry, Paulo Moutinho, Hermann Oliveira Rodrigues, Maria Bowman, Steve Schwartzman, Oriana Almeida, and Sergio Rivero. "The costs and benefits of reducing carbon emissions from deforestation and forest degradation in the Brazilian Amazon". Woods Hole Research Center, December 2007, available from <http://whrc.org/BaliReports/assets/WHRC_Amazon_REDD.pdf> (accessed 2 January 2008).

Nordhaus, William. "The Challenge of Global Warming: Economic Models and Environmental Policy". Mimeographed. Yale University, September 2007*a*.

———. "A Review of the Stern Review on the Economics of Climate Change". *Journal of Economic Literature* XLV (September 2007*b*): 686–702.

Rudd, Kevin. "Ratifying the Kyoto Protocol". Transcript of media release, 3 December 2007, available from <http://www.pm.gov.au/news/releases/2007/media_release_00003.cfm> (accessed 2 January 2008).

Smith, Joel B., Hans-Joachim Schellnhuber, and M. Monirul Qader Mirza. "Chapter 19: Vulnerability to Climate Change and Reasons for Concern: A Synthesis". In IPCC [Intergovernmental Panel on Climate Change], *Climate Change 2001: Impacts, Adaptation and Vulnerability: Contribution of Working Group II to the Third Assessment Report of the Intergovernmental Panel on Climate Change*, edited by James J. McCarthy, Osvaldo F. Canziani, Neil A. Leary, David J. Dokken, and Kasey S. White. Cambridge: Cambridge University Press, 2001.

Stainforth, D., T. Aina, C. Christensen, M. Collins, N. Faull, D.J. Frame, J.A. Kettleborough, S. Knight, A. Martin, J.M. Murphy, C. Piani, D. Sexton, L.A. Smith, R.A. Spicer, A.J. Thorpe, and M.R. Allen. "Uncertainty in Predictions of the Climate Response to Rising Levels of Greenhouse Gases". *Nature* 433 (January 2005): 403–06.

Stern, Nicholas. "On the Specification of Models of Optimum Income Taxation". *Journal of Public Economics* 6 (1976): 123–62.

———. "The Marginal Valuation of Income". In *Studies in Modern Economic Analysis: The Proceedings of the Association of University Teachers of Economics, Edinburgh 1976*, edited by M.J. Artis and A.R. Nobay. Oxford: Basil Blackwell, 1977.

————. *The Economics of Climate Change: The Stern Review*. Cambridge: Cambridge University Press, 2007.

Stern, Nicholas, Jean-Jacques Dethier, and F. Halsey Rogers. *Growth and Empowerment: Making Development Happen*. Cambridge MA: MIT Press, 2005.

Tyndall, John. "On the Absorption and Radiation of Heat by Gases and Vapours". *Philosophical Magazine* 4 (1861): 169–94, 273–85.

UNDP [United Nations Development Program]. *Human Development Report 2007/2008: Fighting Climate Change: Human Solidarity in a Divided World*. New York: United Nations Development Program, 2007.

Chapter 7

THE CHANGING POLITICS OF RELIGIOUS KNOWLEDGE IN ASIA
The Case of Indonesia

John T. Sidel

KNOWLEDGE AND POWER IN THE PROFANE WORLD OF ASIAN POLITICS

At the LSE Asia Forum conference on "The Politics of Knowledge" in Singapore in April 2008, economists, lawyers, sociologists, and other specialists spoke eloquently about the complex issues arising out of the 'Information Economy', the dramatic expansion of education, and the deepening technological challenges facing Asia and the rest of the world in this era of rapid climate change. As for myself, a political scientist and Southeast Asia specialist by training, I spoke of something rather different, something often overlooked in discussions of Knowledge and Power.

In the profane world of politics, 'Knowledge is Power' seems like something of an empty slogan, at least if we consider recent and ongoing trends in much of Asia. Indeed, for all the spread of information via the Internet and the expansion of education in Asia over the past decade, little seems to have changed in terms of the broad structures of political power in the region. Communist parties remain in power in Beijing, Hanoi, Pyongyang, and Vientiane (and arguably Phnom Penh as well). The LDP has weathered splits and challenges in Japan; UMNO is facing challenges in Malaysia, but the People's Action Party (PAP) remains firmly in the saddle in Singapore. For all the in-depth investigative reporting on corruption in India and Indonesia, the Philippines, Taiwan, and Thailand, Asian democracies are still dominated by the politics of machinery and money. For all the ease with which images of state violence are transmitted around the globe, the generals are still in power in Burma (and, in considerable measure, in Pakistan).

Overall, the style of rule may have changed, but not the substance. For the vast majority of people in Asia, it appears, Knowledge does *not* bring Power, just greater — and, at times, more painful — knowledge of powerlessness. In Asia, the powerful may be more knowledgeable than ever before, with more Ph.Ds. among the region's presidents and prime ministers and with rapidly evolving government capacities for gathering knowledge — and thus exerting power — *vis-à-vis* the ever-changing societies across the continent. Today 'Expert' is better than 'Red' in the China of the trained engineer and Tsinghua University graduate Hu Jintao. Daddy (or Grandpa), as it were, still claims to know best. For most people in Asia most of the time, however, the old saw still applies: it's not what you know, it's whom you know.

Viewed against this backdrop, there is little to say about dramatic changes in the constellation of Knowledge and Power in Asia. But if the so-called Information Age has yet to produce dramatic change in the profane world of politics in Asia, the realm of sacral, spiritual power — religion — in the region, as in many other corners of the globe, is today in the throes of a Great Transformation. Established ecclesiastical hierarchies and church structures are in crisis, their hegemonies under threat. Even as political power has remained stubbornly fixed and concentrated in the same few hands in most Asian countries, the established structures of religious knowledge and authority have come to face new challenges and new rival claimants as well. New forms of religious participation and representation are in evidence in a much freer and more pluralistic field of spiritual activity. What the profane world seems to be lacking in political dynamism, diversity, and creativity, the religious world appears to have in abundance. It is no exaggeration to speak of tectonic shifts in the politics of religious knowledge, or, to borrow a term from the profane world of politics, the democratization of religion.

THE DEMOCRATIZATION OF RELIGION: SACRED KNOWLEDGE AND POWER IN FLUX

This pattern of religious democratization is evident in at least three ways. First of all, economic, social, and political change has reduced some of the formal and informal restrictions upon religious life in parts of Communist Asia.[1] In China and Vietnam, in particular, market expansion, economic growth, and the opening of electoral competition for local (i.e. village-level) government posts over the past two decades have all spurred a tremendous religious boom. Local officials and businessmen keen on establishing themselves as good patrons have donated vast sums to build and support temples and pagodas in villages across the Communist heartland. Scholars working in Chinese provinces as diverse as Shaanxi in the north and Fujian in the south have reported that hundreds of thousands of new or newly renovated temples have sprung up in these provinces, with most villages sporting a plurality of sites of worship.[2] These temples "sponsor and 'stage' a wide range of folk cultural activities such as performances by folk dance troupes, music bands and storytellers, folk opera, 'offering presentation' processions, animal sacrifices, and temple festivals".[3] Scholars working in Vietnam have likewise described a similar trend:

> Most homes display a profusion of religious imagery and ritual altars. Temples and Buddhist pagodas are near to overflowing on the first and fifteenth of each lunar month, and are even more crowded at Tet, the Vietnamese New Year celebration. Altars are piled high with offerings; interiors are thick with incense. On the roads one can see devotees returning from offering prayers; they carry ornate rods of smoking incense, flowers, fruit, and other blessings from the gods who watch over their existence. Festivals to honor the spirits of the country's celebrated historical personages attract enormous crowds.

> Ceremonies honouring tutelary deities in village communal houses have undergone a revival after years of restrictions, and expenditure at religious festivals, fairs, and feasts is increasing dramatically. Vast amounts of time and money are being invested in the construction and restoration of religious edifices, from temples, Buddhist pagodas, and Catholic churches down to the lowly shrines to wandering ghosts. Sales of Taiwanese mass-produced images of Ong Dia (the earth god), Than Tai (the god of wealth), and Quan Am (the goddess of mercy) are booming, and all manner of entrepreneurs are selling religious goods and services from paper offerings to the dead to mediumistic and divinatory services.[4]

Meanwhile, beyond the proliferation of spirit mediums and sites of worship in localities around China and Vietnam, trans-local forms of religious activity and association are likewise expanding. Some shrines in Vietnam are said to attract more than one million pilgrims each every year, with their counterparts throughout China no doubt drawing even more spectacular numbers. Buddhists, Catholics, and Protestants, as well as indigenous religious 'cults' like Vietnam's Cao Dai and Hoa Hao continue to outgrow the narrow institutional niches to which they were confined before the onset of market reforms. At the height of its popularity before the crackdown of 1999, the *qigong* group Falun Gong was said to have claimed tens of millions of active participants in its breathing, meditation, and gymnastic exercises across China and beyond into the Chinese diaspora around the world.[5] Overall, then, in countries where official restrictions have long constrained religious practices and encapsulated religious institutions, the expanding exercise of effective religious freedoms over the past two decades has constituted a certain kind of 'democratization of religion', even in the face of repression and under the auspices of entrenched authoritarian rule in the world of profane politics.

Secondly and simultaneously, the past two decades have also witnessed the proliferation of new sources of religious authority, new claimants to religious knowledge, new arbiters of what it means to know God, new interpreters of what it means to be a good Buddhist, Christian, Hindu, or Muslim. Thanks to urbanization and increasing access to communications technology, believers across Asia have a greater ease of access to diverse preachers and prophets, spirit mediums and religious scholars. In cities like Jakarta, Surabaya, and Makassar, a plethora of Sufi and Salafi groups today compete for audiences among millions of Indonesian Muslims,[6] and Islamic 'pop' stars like the famous *da'i* (preacher) Aa Gym reach out to hundreds of thousands if not millions through radio and television appearances, public speaking engagements, cassette, CD, and DVD recordings, and published interviews.[7] In Manila, Cebu, Iloilo, and Davao, El Shaddai and a welter of 'charismatic' Catholic and evangelical Protestant churches vie for the interest of Filipino Christians.

Vincent 'Bingbong' Crisologo's evangelical group The Loved Flock is said to reach 2 million Filipinos by television, while Ramon Orosa's Body of Christ claims a television audience of 3 million, and El Shaddai claims 9–11 million adherents.[8] In Bangkok and beyond, popular monks and monasteries have achieved cult-like status among segments of Thailand's Theravada Buddhist population.[9] Elsewhere in Asia, the sources of religious knowledge are likewise continuing to multiply.

This pluralization of religious authority structures has had a number of important consequences. Most obviously, this trend has eroded the centralized monopolies of the Catholic Church in the Philippines and the *sangha* in Thailand, the privileged position of Nahdlatul Ulama and Muhammadiyah, the two main Islamic associations in Indonesia, and likewise threatened countless other religious establishments across the diverse religious landscape of Asia. Asian Christians, Buddhists, and Muslims thus have come to enjoy increasing freedom of choice in terms of competing sources of religious knowledge they can rely upon, and rival interpretations, methods of interpretation, and modes of applications with regard to such religious knowledge. As one scholar of Hinduism in India noted: "Given the vast array of gurus in India's teeming urban spiritual supermarket, each with his or her own distinctive message and style of relating to devotees, individuals on the lookout for a guru are forced to make active and careful choices from among the countless alternatives available for their ready sampling."[10] The impact of this freedom of choice is evident not only in the emergence of new claimants to religious authority and the movement of adherents from old religious establishments to new ones (and movement of adherents between rivals among them), but also in the efforts of the old religious establishments to adapt to these competitive pressures. Thus Filipino bishops have agreed to recognize "Brother Mike"

Velarde's El Shaddai movement as still belonging to the Catholic Church, Thai *sangha* patriarchs have come to accommodate themselves to questionable teachings and practices by charismatic monks, and leaders of Nahdlatul Ulama and Muhammadiyah have learnt to live with an increasingly diverse field of liberals and leftists, fundamentalists and feminists, Sufi mystics and *salafi* militants competing to interpret, inculcate, and through local experiments in *shari'a* law, implement various understandings of the Islamic faith. With new churches, temples, and mosques springing up left and right, and new preachers and prophets appearing if not on every street corner then on new radio frequencies, television channels, and Internet sites, the threat and practice of religious 'exit' by the faithful thus exerts decidedly downward, democratizing pressures on the established ecclesiastical hierarchies of Asia.

Meanwhile, a third dimension of religious democratization is also evident in the widening forms of popular participation and the shifting patterns of clerical mediation in religious life in various parts of Asia. This pattern is perhaps most visibly evident in the emphasis on the Holy Spirit and on direct religious experience over formal doctrine found in evangelical Protestant groups and in the 'charismatic' Catholic group El Shaddai in the Philippine archipelago. El Shaddai runs wildly popular outdoor prayer meetings in parks and stadiums in Manila and other Philippine cities, even as charismatic Catholic groups convene for sing-along sessions in homes around the archipelago, and rival religious radio and television stations reach out to millions of the faithful on the airwaves. As one observer of El Shaddai's outdoor prayer meetings notes: "In contrast to the mainstream Filipino Catholic religious experience — where the priest and the church building itself mediate with God and the religious community — El Shaddai members, through experience that is largely mass mediated, feel they have a more intimate and immediate (that is, unmediated) relationship with God and their religious community."[11]

Such trends are also amply evident among Asians of other faiths in other settings. In Muslim countries across Asia, written sources of Islamic knowledge — in vernacular Bengali, Indonesian, Malay, and Urdu — are ever more accessible to individual interpretation and analysis. With urbanization, mass literacy, and increasing access to modern means of communication, independent study has increasingly come to supplement or substitute for lessons in the classroom and sermons in the mosque. In the words of Olivier Roy:

> Fragmentary modern knowledge, acquired autodidactically, is integrated within a Quranic intellectual framework, developing, on the one hand, the image of a transcendent totality, the *tawhid* (the oneness of God, which extends to His Creation), in which all knowledge comes together, and, on the other hand, a terminology drawn from the Tradition, supported by the citation of verses, but often positioned as the equivalent of concepts issued from modern ideologies. The two bodies of knowledge (modern through brochures and manuals, Quranic by citation) in fact cover a 'do-it-yourself' creation, the juxtaposition of segments of knowledge into a whole whose logic cannot be reduced to the sum of its parts.[12]

Indeed, millions of Asian Muslims from Indonesia to Pakistan spend hours each week surfing the Internet, visiting diverse Islamic websites, chatrooms, and blogspots and consulting multiple *fatāwā* and online versions of Al-Qur'an.[13] At the same time, access to esoteric forms of Islamic mysticism is likewise broadening. In Indonesia, for example, beyond the established Sufi orders or *tarekat* (Arabic: *tariqa*, plural: *turuq*), "Sufism has been adapted to a variety of new institutional forms in urban settings. Some of them build out from classic institutions like the *pengajian* or *tarekat*, but modify them substantially; others utilize such international cultural forms as the 'foundation,' 'institute,' 'seminar series,' 'intensive course,' or 'spiritual workshop' ".[14]

Parallel trends are reported by scholars of Hinduism in contemporary India. On the one hand, direct access to mass media has made for new forms of direct Hindu devotion. As one study of the impact of the mass media on Hinduism in India concluded: "television produces the effect of a free and unconditional viewing experience, and insinuates a sense of costless social intimacy: the presence of a stream of ongoing communication lends itself to viewers' imaginative participation without necessarily enfolding them in networks of dependence."[15] On the other hand, there is evidence of shifts in the role of gurus in "transmitting authoritative spiritual knowledge" among hundreds of millions of Indian Hindus.[16] Increasing numbers of Indian Hindus, it is reported, are attracted to high-profile modern guru organizations because of the *"personal freedom* to create for oneself a religious life conducive to one's particular individual tastes and dispositions and the possibilities for *"self-authorship* of a highly personalized form of religious faith...personally constructed by the individual concerned to suit his specific inclinations and requirements. In constructing this personalized religion, the individual makes selections from a wide array of elements that he or she encounters in his/her religious environment".[17]

Thus overall, for Asian believers no longer content to sit quietly on church pews, in *madrasa* classrooms or on the floors and steps of temples and ashrams listening to sermons or religious lessons, more active, unmediated forms of participation in religious life and more autodidactic forms of religious education are ever more readily available. It is not only that believers have greater choice from among an increasing plurality of sources of religious knowledge, but that they also play a much more active, unmediated role in the process of acquiring religious knowledge themselves. As one scholar of popular religion in Vietnam concluded:

> Some paths lead to Buddhist pagodas, Christian churches, and temples to protector spirits, where a person might enter into dealings with one or several of the images found there.... As they negotiate this complex symbolic world, adepts consult with any manner of astrologers, geomancers, physiognomists, fortune-tellers, mediums, monks, sorcerers, and temple custodians. Their itineraries are not predetermined by any religious order and are virtually impossible for the state to regulate. Rather, people's belief and practices are influenced by family, neighbours, colleagues, business clients, fellow worshipers, religious entrepreneurs, and popular publications. Believers exchange stories about the potency of different spirits, hearing of miraculous events and learning new solutions to their problems from those encountered along their way.
>
> *In this non-institutionalized fund of advice, interpretation, and creative usage, novel interpretations are constantly being made; a syncretic ferment is continually on the brew.*[18]

Overall, these three trends can be understood as liberating ones with regard to established patterns of control over religious knowledge throughout much of Asia over the past two decades. Today, more and more Asians enjoy greater freedom to acquire religious knowledge, greater access to diverse sources of religious knowledge, and greater capacity to acquire, accumulate, and actively enjoy and articulate religious knowledge themselves. If not quite a 'World Turned Upside Down', the religious landscape of Asia is one in which the steep hierarchies of authority are increasingly challenged and contested by rival sources and sites of religious knowledge, and in which greater freedom of choice, of exit, and of voice is ever more evident. In this sense, then, we can speak of the democratization of religion in Asia, a trend not paralleled in the realm of profane politics.

RELIGIOUS KNOWLEDGE, POWER, AND VIOLENCE: THE CASE OF INDONESIA

Viewed in this perspective, the various forms of religious violence observed in Asia in recent years — inter-religious pogroms in India and Indonesia, Islamist terrorism from Islamabad to Bali — can be understood in a new light. With the decay of old religious monopolies, the breakdown of old religious boundaries, and the unmooring of religious identities from old anchors, religious democratization has produced unsettling uncertainties. Uncertainties for millions of believers, and uncertainties for those long accustomed to speaking with enforceable authority about what makes a good Buddhist, Christian, Hindu, or Muslim and to claiming privileged or exclusive knowledge about Buddhism, Christianity, Hinduism, or Islam. In the face of such uncertainties, small wonder that a desperate minority sometimes turns to violence in the name of an embattled version of the faith.

Indeed, it is precisely the democratization of religion that has provided a backdrop to episodes of violence in the name of one or another faith in various parts of Asia over the past two decades. Such violence has sometimes taken the form of secular state crackdowns on unauthorized religious practices and organizations in countries like China and Vietnam, or official religious institutions' efforts to discipline and punish wayward members of their putative flocks, as seen at times in Malaysia, or counterinsurgency campaigns against movements arising from among religious minorities outgrowing established forms of institutional representation, encapsulation, and domestication, as in the southern Muslim provinces of Thailand and the Philippines. In addition, such violence has also at times assumed the form of violent inter-religious conflict, in contexts of both democratization in the profane realm of politics and heightened uncertainty and flux with regard to the structures of religious authority and identity, as seen in India and Indonesia.

This pattern is evident in the case of the rising incidence of anti-Muslim violence in India over the past two decades with the breakdown of Congress one-party rule in the country.[19] On the one hand, as suggested above, this trend has reflected not increasing clarity and uniformity as to what it means to be a Hindu, but rather growing diversity and choice in terms of Hindu gurus and guru organizations.[20] On the other hand, as scholars have argued, this trend has reflected not deepening solidarities among Hindus and deference to Hindu hierarchies of spiritual authority, but rather the spreading threat and practice of conflict among Hindus, with lower-caste mobilization in elections and otherwise threatening higher-caste domination like never before. These trends, scholars have argued, have encouraged politicians associated with Hindu 'nationalist' parties like the BJP to engage in inter-religious hate-mongering and scapegoating, and to encourage and enable collective violence against Muslims as a means of countering perceived threats to 'Hindutva' and firming up the structures of Hindu authority and identity.[21]

Meanwhile, the case of Indonesia offers a somewhat different example of the connection between democratization and inter-religious violence. Indonesia, after all, has witnessed a complex pattern of rising and then declining violence in the name of Islam in tandem with the process of transition from authoritarian rule over the past decade. This pattern first manifested itself in the final years of the Soeharto era (1995–97) in a series of religious riots, in which crowds of Islamic students initiated attacks on ethnic-Chinese business establishments, non-Muslim houses of worship, and government buildings in the aftermath of incidents involving perceived slights or insults against Islam. With the fall of Soeharto in May 1998, these riots faded from view and were replaced, as it were, by a series of inter-religious pogroms in 1999–2001, in which Christians and Muslims attacked neighbourhoods and villages across the religious divide in localities in the provinces of Maluku, North Maluku, and Central Sulawesi. Even as these pogroms began to peter out, other forms of violence in the name of religion emerged, now articulated in the idiom of *jihad*. Thus April 2000 saw the formation of a paramilitary group called Laskar Jihad and its deployment to defend Muslims and attack Christians in areas of inter-religious conflict, and Christmas Eve 2000 saw a series of terrorist bombings of Christian churches around the archipelago (in retribution for major atrocities against Muslim communities by armed Christian groups a year earlier). In October 2002, moreover, a series of explosions in Bali marked the onset of a globalized terrorist campaign in Indonesia, with foreigners targeted again in bombings in Jakarta in 2003 and 2004, and in Bali once again in 2005. Most recently, just as these annual detonations ceased, evidence of a return to the pattern of the mid-1990s came into view, with a wave of attacks by groups like the 'Front for the Defenders of Islam' (Front Pembela Islam) on Protestant churches and 'deviant' Ahmadiyya mosques in different parts of the country.[22]

This pattern of rising and declining violence in the name of Islam reflected shifts in the structures of religious authority in Indonesia and a set of uncertainties and anxieties regarding hierarchies and boundaries of control over the production of religious knowledge in the country amidst all the sea changes accompanying democratization. In Indonesia, after all, the 1990s had seen the rise to public prominence of new efforts to combine knowledge and power in the name of religion, most obviously in the case of Islam, during a period of transition from authoritarian rule in the country. The long years of the Soeharto era had served to promote the dramatic expansion of Islamic education in Indonesia. The school networks associated with the 'traditionalist' Nahdlatul Ulama (NU) and the 'modernist' Muhammadiyah expanded horizontally to attract more and more students, and vertically to include tertiary education, through their own separate sets of universities, and to feed into the fourteen branches of the State Islamic Institute (IAIN) as well as mainstream state universities, previously dominated by non-Muslims and Muslims with no religious education. By the 1990s, mainstream state universities throughout Indonesia saw a marked rise in the numbers of students with devout Muslim backgrounds and in the popularity of campus mosques, prayer and religious discussion groups, and Islamic student organizations.[23] As one observer noted: "Mosques are filled with worshipers, particularly young adults; *halaqah* and *pengajian* emerge in almost every university complex and neighbourhood; extra religious schooling (*diniyah*) in the afternoon is crowded with children and teens; the circulation of Islamic books has reached the highest point in Indonesian history; and female students and adults with head-coverings have become a regular phenomenon on campuses and public places."[24]

By this time, three decades of sustained economic growth, urbanization, and the extension of the tertiary educational sector had thus also begun to bring into the ranks of the educated urban middle class an unprecedented number of Muslims coming from backgrounds of Islamic piety and learning. This trend was evident in the prominence of devout, mostly modernist, Muslims in the business world, on university campuses, in the mass media, and, increasingly, in the armed forces, the bureaucracy, and other power centres within the state — preserves previously dominated by Christians and Muslims with little to no formal schooling in their faith.

The creation of ICMI, the All-Indonesian Association of Islamic Intellectuals, in 1990, worked to recognize and reinforce this trend. With Soeharto's long-time close associate B.J. Habibie as its chairman, ICMI came to serve as an important network for recruitment into the political class and as a generously endowed source of patronage. Under its auspices, moreover, support for 'Muslim professionals' was fairly matched by promotion of 'professional Muslims', through ICMI backing for a diverse range of Islamic publishing, preaching, and associational activities. Embedded within the authoritarian state, and enjoying unprecedented and unparalleled opportunities for state promotion of 'Islam', ICMI gave great sustenance and hope to those Islamist activists concerned to overcome Indonesia's famous diversity of Islamic practices and organizations, and to promote a modernist, reified notion of Islam not contaminated or compromised by parochialism, syncretism, or the pluralism of educational traditions and associational life of the vast Indonesian archipelago. Thus the resignation of Soeharto and the immediate assumption of the presidency by then vice-president Habibie in May 1998 represented the triumph of the 'Islamic Trend' in Indonesia.[25]

With the elections of June 1999, however, the fiction of a united Muslim population universally represented by ICMI dissipated with fragmentation and factionalism among a welter of Islamic parties, and dissolved in the face of strong electoral showings by non-Islamist parties among Muslim and non-Muslim voters alike. Indeed, a clear plurality of the vote (34 per cent) was won by Megawati Soekarnoputri's Indonesian Democratic Party of Struggle (Partai Demokrasi Indonesia — Perjuangan or PDI-P), a party known for its ecumenical, and 'syncretist' orientation, and sizeable non-Muslim constituencies and membership. More than one-third of the members of parliament elected on the PDI-P ticket were non-Muslims (mostly Protestants), and virtually none of its Muslim MPs claimed a background of Islamic education or associational activity.[26] By contrast, parties with avowedly Islamic agendas achieved less than 20 per cent of the vote, while the Partai Amanat Nasional (National Mandate Party) led by the modernist Muslim association Muhammadiyah's chairman Amien Rais won 8 per cent under an ostensibly ecumenical banner and with token non-Muslims in its ranks. The universalistic claims made under the sign of 'Islam' were fully revealed as partisan, particularistic, and rather poorly received even among the broad mass of the Muslim population. Thus October 1999 saw the replacement of Habibie as president by Abdurrahman Wahid, head of the National Awakening Party (PKB), long-time chairman of the 'traditionalist' Nahdlatul Ulama and persistent champion of inter-faith tolerance and cooperation; Wahid was subsequently succeeded in mid-2001 by the PDI-P's Megawati Soekarnoputri, who in turn fell in the 2004 elections to Indonesia's current president, the retired Army general Susilo Bambang Yudhoyono.

Overall, the years since the brief Habibie interlude of May 1998 – October 1999 have witnessed the unfolding of trends which attest to the diminution, demobilization, and domestication of Islamist forces in Indonesia. This shift is evident if one considers the failed efforts of Islamist parties in 1999–2002 to insert references to Islamic law into the Constitution, and the subsequent acquiescence of these parties in the reaffirmation of the ecumenical, if insistently monotheistic, principles of *Pancasila* for the parameters of social and political life in the country.[27]

This shift is likewise apparent if one compares the prominence and power of modernist and puritanical strains in Indonesian Islam in 1998–99 with the subsequent political triumphs of traditionalist Muslim, ecumenical, and even Christian elements in political contests in Jakarta, and with broader societal trends.

Indeed, the past several years have seen the flourishing of diverse forms of religious expression and associational activity within the broad realm of Indonesian Islam, which is world famous for its diversity, its organizational pluralism, its syncretic tendencies, and its engagement with the secularizing forces of the capitalist market and the modern state. Journalists have tracked the rising popularity of Sufi brotherhoods and of diverse religious cults, both in Jakarta and other major cities, and in the rural hinterlands of the archipelago.[28] The past few years have also witnessed the rise of new charismatic *kyai* (religious scholars) who enjoy unprecedented popularity outside established Islamic associational hierarchies, thanks to the appeal of their mystical, Sufistic, and 'supernatural' approaches.[29] Meanwhile, unofficial religious groups which have long existed on the fringes of the permissible have begun to press for more official recognition of their de facto authority over sizeable flocks of the faithful.[30] Scholars tracing these trends have written of the increasing "permeability in the boundaries of the nation's official religions", and the "emergence of an arena of unregulated 'spiritual' groups that now exists along the highly regulated, rigidly denominational religious market structured by the New Order Government (1996–1998)."[31] Overall, the existing hierarchies of Islamic worship and learning in Indonesia are today facing unprecedented difficulties in maintaining their authority over the diverse population of 200 million Muslims across the archipelago.

Meanwhile, the unfolding of political and social liberalization, democratization, and decentralization in the years since the fall of Soeharto in 1998, as well as the economic recovery and growth experienced in the aftermath of the deep financial crisis of the same year, have drawn millions of Indonesians into forms of identity, activity, and association which compete with those offered by Islam. Thus recent years have seen the revival of ethnic and regional identities, the re-emergence of *adat* (customary law) and aristocratic lineages in local politics, and a modest resurgence of labour activism, all at the expense of efforts to promote a streamlined, standardized, universalistic Islam. At the same time, against these centrifugal tendencies towards fragmentation along regional, ethnic, and class lines, the centripetal force of the revitalized Indonesian economy has continued to attract millions of Indonesian Muslims to patterns of consumption — of clothing, technology, and entertainment — that also work to pull them away from religious piety. Under conditions of unprecedented liberalization, the Indonesian entertainment industry — from movies to radio and television soap operas, romance novels to pop music — is highly vibrant today, as producer of domestic content and transmitter of global popular culture.

It is against this broad backdrop that the efforts of various Islamist politicians and parties in recent years to reassert their power in public life in Indonesia and their control over the production and circulation of religious knowledge in the country must be situated. The quasi-governmental Council of Indonesian Islamic Scholars (Majelis Ulama Indonesia or MUI), for example, has in recent years issued a series of controversial *fatwa* (Arabic: *fatāwā*) including one condemning "pluralism, secularism, and liberalism" and another denouncing as heretical the Ahmadiyah sect.[32] But these *fatwa* are neither legally binding nor representative of the elected government's policies and preferences.[33] Indeed, the issuance of these fatwa has provoked considerable controversy in the Indonesian press, with prominent Islamic figures like former president and Nahdlatul Ulama chairman Abdurrahman

Wahid condemning the edicts and calling for the abolition of the MUI.

These MUI *fatwa*, it is worth noting, reflect the increasing difficulties experienced by those trying to retain — or rather, to regain — a measure of control over the production and circulation of Islamic knowledge in Indonesia. After all, the MUI *fatwa* against "pluralism, secularism, and liberalism" was issued against the backdrop of a consolidated Indonesian democracy, in which pluralism is alive and well, not only in terms of political parties competing for public offices, but also in the realm of religious associational, educational, and devotional life. This *fatwa* was issued against the backdrop of a recovering Indonesian economy whose deepening integration into global markets has been accompanied by the increasing availability and consumption of images, products, and services whose origins are utterly secular in nature. This *fatwa* was issued against the backdrop of the ongoing liberalization of Indonesian society, in terms of the expansion of individual freedoms in all realms of social life. This *fatwa* was issued by a body lacking in official juridical authority or effective capacity for enforcement, a body forced to compete for Muslim hearts and minds with newly formed groups like the Liberal Islam Network (Jaringan Islam Liberal or JIL), whose activities and publications are generously funded by U.S.-based foundations.

Another example of efforts to reassert control over what it means to be a good Muslim in Indonesia lies in the realm of attempts to restrict the public visibility and freedom of women in the country. For example, the publication of a new Indonesian edition of Playboy magazine in April 2006 was met by vehement condemnation in the press — and angry protests in the streets — by various Islamist groups, even though the editors had decided not to include nude centerfolds or other photos of naked women as had originally been anticipated.[34] Early 2006 also saw the eruption of controversy over legislation proposed by Islamist parties ostensibly to restrict pornography in Indonesia, but introducing broad regulations on women's dress and behaviour in public.[35] Alongside this controversy came well-publicized attacks by Islamist groups against a highly popular Indonesian dancer, whose allegedly sensual gyrations had earned her a considerable live and video audience, and whose own cafes and nightclubs in Jakarta had attracted a growing clientele.[36]

These episodes revealed the difficulties faced by those trying to reassert control over understandings of Islam and of appropriately 'Islamic' notions of gender and sexuality. As many authors have noted, Islamist groups in diverse settings have long been preoccupied with the exercise of social control over women, treating them, in the words of the eminent Middle East specialist Charles Tripp, "as the terrain for the symbolic expression of a certain kind of Islamic identity, but also as key players in the defence against the intrusion of other belief systems."[37]

> Echoing contemporary secular nationalist discourses, there is stress on the functional role of women in maintaining and reproducing a distinctively Islamic society, through the act of giving birth and educating children. The security of the domestic environment becomes the guarantee of a truly Islamic society, since it is the site for the production of the strong 'Islamic personality' who does battle with the world in the service of Islamic values. This places a heavy historical and sociological responsibility on women, making their comportment and actions a matter for general concern by the largely male cohort of concerned Muslim intellectuals.[38]

Indeed, in Indonesia the issue of Muslim women's attire had long been a focus of Islamist activists' attention and political agitation, most notably in the late 1980s and early 1990s, when the government's long-standing prohibition on Islamic headscarves in state schools was overturned in favour of permissiveness and encouragement.[39]

This Islamist concern to restrict and regulate women's behaviour and comportment in public life must be understood in the context of the increasing mobility of women in Indonesian society in recent decades.[40] Already in the Soeharto era, economic growth, industrialization, and urbanization had brought millions of Indonesian women out of the homes and villages of the country and into factory belts, supermarkets and department stores, and, in smaller numbers, universities, from which a range of urban professional opportunities were opened up to them.[41] With recovery from the economic crisis of 1997–98, these trends have resumed in the post-Soeharto era. With every passing year, more Indonesian women are travelling farther from home, working in industrial and service jobs, joining the ranks of the civil service and the professional classes, and exercising more choice over their movements, the use of their labour power and their money, and their modes of communication and expression than ever before.[42] The creation of the Ministry for the Empowerment of Women represents the government's belated recognition of — and reaction to — these trends, even as the growing ranks and range of activities of women's organizations attached to Muhammadiyah and Nahdlatul Ulama attest to the accommodating response of mainstream Islamic groups in Indonesia.[43]

Other trends have worked to undermine the conservative understandings of family life and sexuality assiduously promoted by the Soeharto regime over the three decades of its reign.[44] Homosexuality is more visible in the public sphere than ever before, as perhaps best exemplified by the holding of a book launch for a novel about a lesbian love affair at a branch of the

IAIN (Institut Agama Islam Negeri or State Islamic Institute) in late 2003.[45] As Dédé Oetomo, Indonesia's best known openly gay public figure, has noted, there is "a greatly increased public awareness of the variety of human sexualities… True, many misunderstandings remain, but they are eroding."[46] Small wonder that male Islamist activists — and other men anxious about the weakening hold of conservative patterns of familial authority and gender relations — in Indonesia have tried to reassert various forms of regulatory control over sexuality in public life.

These efforts to shore up certain notions of Islamic propriety and rectitude in Indonesia social life have in some measure been matched in the political realm, with the much ballyhooed rise to prominence of the Partai Keadilan Sejahtera (PKS or Prosperous Justice Party). The party won more than 7 per cent in the 2004 parliamentary elections, placing it above the established National Mandate Party (PAN) of former Muhammadiyah chairman Amien Rais and just behind current president Susilo Bambang Yudhoyono's Democratic Party (Partai Demokrat), with especially strong showings in Jakarta and other major Indonesian cities. Today, former PKS chairman Hidayat Nur Wahid serves as the head of the supra-parliamentary People's Consultative Assembly (Majelis Permusyawaratan Rakyat or MPR), the party is well represented in local assemblies, and PKS-backed candidates have fared well in recent elections for local executive posts as mayors, regents, and governors around the country. Some party activists and other political analysts predict even greater successes for the PKS in the 2009 national elections.[47]

Like many other political parties in the Muslim world identifying themselves in terms of the promotion of 'Justice', 'Prosperity', and 'Welfare', Indonesia's PKS is a decidedly Islamist party in terms of its origins and orientation. Its leadership emerged out of a network of highly pious, puritanical, and politicized university students that evolved over the course of the Soeharto era, linking discussion groups from various campus mosques in the country's top universities as well as Indonesian Muslim students at universities in the Middle East and elsewhere in the world. Even as they pursued doctorates in various technical and scientific fields, these students were attracted to puritanical currents in Islamic thinking and to the organizational and mobilizational techniques developed by Hassan Al-Banna and the Muslim Brotherhood in Egypt since the 1930s.[48]

While this kind of backdrop to the party's emergence and orientation may remind readers of similar — and often similarly named — Islamist parties and movements elsewhere in the Muslim world, whether in Pakistan or Turkey, Egypt or Morocco, the party's actual modus operandi from election campaigning to parliamentary coalition-building is reminiscent of the broad pattern of cooptation, domestication, and transformation of such Islamist parties noted by many observers.[49] The party's appeal among voters, after all, came not from its commitment to the Islamicization of Indonesian state and society, but from a reputation for relative incorruptibility and seriousness of purpose compared to the prevailing patterns of money and machine politics in the country. The nature of this appeal has been evident not only in the party's official name and policy pronouncements, but also in its campaign rallies, which have attracted thousands of clean-shaven men, and headscarf-less women, as the author observed first-hand in both Bandung and Jakarta in the weeks leading up to the 2004 parliamentary elections. After the 2004 elections and the inauguration of the administration of Susilo Bambang Yudhoyono, this emphasis in PKS public relations was evident in the resignation of Hidayat Nur Wahid from the party leadership prior to his elevation to speaker of the MPR, in the party's MPs' rejection of many of the perks of parliamentary office, and in the party's avowedly principled — rather than patronage-based — support for the new president's choice of cabinet ministers.[50]

For skeptics and alarmists, the public profile of the PKS is seen as a thin veneer behind which the 'fundamentalists' running the party have succeeded in luring unsuspecting voters into mistaken support for the party and in lulling other politicians into complacency as the party consolidates its gains and expands its influence. The party's public disavowal of further intentions to seek Islamist amendments to the Constitution, its inclusion of many women — and token non-Muslims — among its internal governing bodies and parliamentary slates, and other such efforts to de-emphasize the party's Islamist origins and orientation are simply duplicitous.[51] Once the party expands its share of the electorate and its influence in parliament and the cabinet in the years to come, the PKS will 'show its true colours' and reveal itself for the extremist, intolerant, fundamentalist party it supposedly remains at heart.[52]

Yet what this interpretation of PKS ignores is the extent to which the party's participation within the parliamentary arena has transformed if not its leaders' conscious sense of commitment to long-term Islamist goals, then their unconscious understanding of the party's short- and medium-term interests *as well as its very identity*. For whatever the PKS leaders may confide amongst themselves, their continuing efforts to promote the party as the vehicle of — essentially secular — 'good governance' in Indonesian politics have reoriented the party's collective activities, its style and language of self-presentation, and its members' everyday practices in a not particularly Islamist direction. Meanwhile, as the party has engaged in behind-the-scenes informal horsetrading and coalition-building with machine politicians of various stripes over recent years, its effective commitment to various high-minded goals — whether 'good governance' or 'Islam' — has been compromised. Thus, like the Christian Democrats in Western Europe before World War I, and the Euro-Communists during the Cold War, the Islamists of today may well be duping themselves more than they are duping others, with parties like Indonesia's PKS effectively embodying gradual Islamist integration and accommodation, willy-nilly, with liberal democracy.[53] Compared to other Islamist parties in the Muslim world, moreover, the PKS seems to lack the kind of densely woven and deeply rooted local infrastructure so carefully nurtured by their counterparts in Egypt and Jordan, Turkey and Pakistan, the Gaza Strip and the West Bank over the years.

This weakness is readily apparent if one considers the broad realm of local politics in Indonesia, which in recent years has featured efforts by Islamic vigilante groups and initiatives to impose Islamic law on localities where they command influence. The impression imparted is one of widespread Islamist activism at the local level throughout Indonesia, with accumulating Islamist momentum 'from below' around the country under conditions of decentralization since the enactment of 'regional autonomy' legislation in 1999. For example, from its formation in mid-1998 during the brief Habibie interlude to this day, the Front for the Defenders of Islam (Front Pembela Islam or FPI) has won considerable media attention for its high-profile campaigns against gambling, prostitution, and alcohol in Jakarta and other cities, its occasional anti-U.S. protests, and its antics as an enforcer of Islamic morality.[54] The year 2005, moreover, saw a series of widely publicized attacks by FPI and other Islamist groups coalescing in an 'anti-apostasy movement' against churches in West Java accused of operating without licences and of attempting to spread Christianity among the Muslim population.[55] Finally, by 2006, press coverage of local politics in Indonesia had begun to focus on the supposedly growing number of regencies where local assemblies had imposed regulations in the name of Islamic law, banning gambling, prostitution, and alcohol, for example, or imposing restrictions on women's dress code and comportment in public.[56] In the province of South Sulawesi alone, at least six of 24 regencies were cited as localities where various forms of *shari'a* law were in place.[57] The case of a young woman detained for alleged 'prostitution' in the Jakarta suburb of Tangerang for being improperly clad while awaiting an evening bus home from work similarly attracted national and international publicity.[58]

Yet overall, the broad pattern of local politics in Indonesia is one in which both inter-religious violence and Islamist influence have largely subsided and been sublimated within the workings of the world's third largest consolidated democracy. Indeed, compared to the preceding decade, the most striking feature of local politics in Indonesia is the relative absence of violence — nothing like the anti-Chinese riots of 1995–97, the widespread mayhem of 1998, or the incidents of communal violence of 1999–2001 has occurred over the past several years.[59] Even in the Central Sulawesi regency of Poso or the provinces of Maluku and Maluku Utara, where inter-religious violence caused a few thousand deaths in 1999–2001, there has been virtually no resurgence of large-scale communal conflict. Indeed, the rising incidence of church burnings documented by concerned Christian groups in the 1990s tapered off and virtually ceased since the turn of the twenty-first century. Overall, the pattern throughout Indonesia is one of accommodation between Muslims and non-Muslims in local politics, as evident in the success of the ecumenical parties GOLKAR and PDIP in the majority of local parliamentary elections and the prevalence of cross-cutting inter-religious coalitions in the elections for local executive posts.

To be sure, Islamic parties like PKS have come to enjoy considerable popularity and influence in certain localities around the country, regional assemblies dominated by Islamist parties have enacted local *shari'a* regulations in a number of localities, and groups like FPI exert more informal forms of influence and intimidation in the name of Islam. Yet the areas — and episodes — of Islamist activism are hardly representative of the broad trends in the vast majority of localities around the vast Indonesian archipelago, with its majority-Muslim population of 225 million people.

Moreover, insofar as the PKS and other Islamic forces have enjoyed some success in local politics in recent years, it is far from clear whether this trend should be viewed narrowly in terms of 'Islamization'. After all, the basis of PKS local appeal — and the focus of its local campaign energies — has been the struggle against local corruption, as embodied in the realm of machine politics dominated by the two largest ecumenical parties, GOLKAR and PDIP.[60] In many provinces, moreover, alongside PKS and other Islamic parties, Islamic university student organizations and other Islamic associational networks have provided virtually the only effective counterweight in civil society to the vast patronage resources and regulatory powers of the state.[61]

At the same time, it seems clear that not all Islamist politics should be taken so seriously in ideological terms: groups like FPI (and their backers and collaborators) have used the threat of violence in the name of Islam for extortionary purposes, and local assemblies' enactment of so-called *shari'a* legislation has likewise served to expand the regulatory powers of the local state, the discretionary privileges of local politicians, and the rent-seeking opportunities of local enforcers. Even in South Sulawesi, where the spread of local *shari'a* regulations appears to be most advanced, knowledgeable observers report that Islamist parties and politicians remain involved in all manner of opportunistic horse-trading and collusion with their non-Islamist counterparts in GOLKAR and PDIP.[62] Overall, then, fitful — and largely failing — efforts to control the production and circulation of religious knowledge in Indonesia, as elsewhere in Asia, are drawn in diverse directions, with the fragmentation of religious authority and the diversification of religious practices and affiliations accompanying democratization, decentralization, liberalization of public life across the archipelago.

DEMOCRATIZING RELIGIOUS KNOWLEDGE AND POWER IN ASIA

Over the course of the past several two decades, countless commentators have treated religious 'resurgence' or 'revival' as a threat to secularism and multi-faith tolerance, with violence in the name of religion first pathologized in terms of 'ethnic conflict' in the 1990s and as 'Islamist terrorism' since September 2001. But such episodes of violence should not blind us to the broadly emancipatory trends observable in religious life throughout much of the world, whose contours have been sketched, however cursorily, with regard to Asia, and in greater depth with regard to the case of Indonesia. Violence has always accompanied democratization in the profane world of politics, and it is unsurprising to find violence alongside what I have called democratization in the realm of religion. Such is the nature of contestation over claims to knowledge and claims to power when it is not fully subordinated to the rules of constitutional democracy.

As argued above, the past two decades have witnessed three broad trends in terms of patterns of control over the production, circulation, and consumption of religious knowledge throughout much of Asia. First of all, the past two decades have seen expanding enjoyment of religious freedoms in Asian contexts where restrictions on religious practice have long been in place, most notably in China and Vietnam. Second, the past two decades have also seen the increasing pluralization of sources of religious authority, sources of knowledge about various faiths and about what it means to be a good Buddhist, Christian, Hindu, or Muslim. Third and finally, the past two decades have witnessed a dramatic expansion in the nature and extent of active participation by Asian believers in the production and reproduction of religious knowledge. In these three senses, then, one can speak of the democratization of religion in Asia, even in the face of continuing authoritarianism and other obstacles to democratization in the realm of profane politics. In all of these senses, the democratization of Islam in Indonesia, the world's most populous majority-Muslim country, is thus well under way, episodes of religious violence notwithstanding.

Beyond these trends, insofar as democratization has proceeded in the profane world of politics, the impact on control over religious knowledge has lain in the direction of increasing contestation and popularization. The expanding realm of electoral politics, by drawing in individuals and institutions in the religious field into competition for electoral offices, has created an alternative basis for the evaluation of claims to religious authority: the popular vote. Here one can see the undeniable, perhaps insurmountable, tension between religious authority and democracy. For the legitimacy of popular sovereignty and the divine commandments of the faith may well be, at some level, ultimately incommensurable and irreconcilable. As the avowedly atheist author Julian Barnes writes:

> A common response in surveys of religious attitudes is to say something like, 'I don't go to church, but I have my own

personal idea of God.' This kind of statement makes me in turn react like a philosopher. Soppy, I cry. You may have your own personal idea of God, but does God have His own personal idea of you? Because that's what matters. Whether He's an old man with a white beard sitting in the sky, or a life force, or a disinterested prime mover, or a clockmaker, or a woman, or a nebulous moral force, or Nothing At All, what counts is what He, She, It or Nothing thinks of you rather than you of them. The notion of redefining the deity into something that works for you is grotesque. It also doesn't matter whether God is just or benevolent or even observant — of which there seems to be startlingly little proof — only that He exists.[63]

There may be limits to the democratization of religion, but religions still have an important role to play in this worldly struggles for freedom in Asia and beyond, even if, as the philosopher Charles Taylor has argued, we live in "a Secular Age."[64] As events on the streets of Rangoon last fall have suggested, the processes of democratic change in the religious realm inevitably spill over into the profane world of politics, despite the assiduous efforts of those in power to master and manipulate religious institutions and symbols in the service of the status quo. In the decades ahead, new forms of religious knowledge will gradually help to create new forms of politics and new constellations of power in Asia as elsewhere in the world.

Notes

1. Pitman B. Potter, "Belief in Control: Regulation of Religion in China", *China Quarterly* 174 (2003): 317–37.

2. See, for example, Adam Yuet Chan, *Miraculous Response: Doing Popular Religion in China* (Stanford: Stanford University Press, 2006) and Kenneth Dean, "Local Communal religion in Contemporary Southeast China", *China Quarterly* 174 (2003): 341.

3. Chan, *Miraculous Response*, p. 2.

4. Philip Taylor, *Goddess on the Rise: Pilgrimage and Popular Religion in Vietnam* (Honolulu: University of Hawai'i Press, 2004), pp. 1–2.

5. Vivienne Shue, "Global Imaginings, the State's Quest for Hegemony, and the Pursuit of Phantom Freedom in China: From Heshang to Falun Gong", in *Globalization and Democratization in Asia: The Construction of Identity*, edited by Catarina Kinnvall and Kristina Jonsson (London: Routledge, 2002), pp. 210–29; James Tong, "An Organizational Analysis of the *Falun Gong*: Structure, Communications, Financing", *China Quarterly* 171 (2002): 636–60; and David A. Palmer, *Qigong Fever: Body, Science and Utopia in China* (New York: Columbia University Press, 2007).

6. Michael Laffan, "National Crisis and the Representation of Traditional Sufism in Indonesia: The Periodicals *Salafy* and *Sufi*", and Julia Day Howell, "Modernity and Islamic Spirituality in Indonesia's New Sufi Networks", in *Sufism and the 'Modern' in Islam*, edited by Martin van Bruinessen and Julia Day Howell (London: I.B. Tauris, 2007), pp. 149–71, 217–40.

7. Patrick Haenni, *L'islam de marché: L'autre révolution conservatrice* (Paris: Seuil, 2005).

8. For such estimates, see Paul Freston, *Evangelicals and Politics in Asia, Africa, and Latin America* (Cambridge: Cambridge University Press, 2001).

9. See, for example, Peter A. Jackson, "The Enchanting Spirit of Thai Capitalism: The Cult of Luang Phor Khoon and the Post-Modernization of Thai Buddhism", *South East Asia Research* 7, no. 1 (March 1999).

10. Maya Warrier, "Processes of Secularization in Contemporary India: Guru Faith in the Mata Amritanandamayi Mission", *Modern Asian Studies* 37, no. 1 (February 2003).

11. Katharine L. Wiegele, *Investing in Miracles: El Shaddai and the Transformation of Popular Catholicism in the Philippines* (Honolulu: University of Hawai'i Press, 2005).

12. Olivier Roy, *The Failure of Political Islam* (Cambridge: Harvard University Press, 1994).

13. For early accounts of these trends, see Gary R. Bunt, *Virtually Islamic: Computer-Mediated Communication and Cyber Islamic Environments* (Cardiff: University of Wales Press, 2000); and Gary R. Bunt, *Islam in the Digital Age: E-Jihad, Online Fatwas and Cyber Islamic Environments* (London: Pluto Press, 2003).

14. Julia Day Howell, "Sufism and the Indonesian Islamic Revival", *Journal of Asian Studies* 60, no. 3 (August 2001).

15. Arvind Rajagopal, *Politics After Television: Religious Nationalism and the Reshaping of the Indian Public* (Cambridge: Cambridge University Press, 2001).

16. Lise McKean, *Divine Enterprise: Gurus and the Hindu Nationalist Movement* (Chicago: University of Chicago Press, 1996).

17. Warrier, "Processes of Secularization in Contemporary India", pp. 231–32.

18. Philip Taylor, *Goddess on the Rise: Pilgrimage and Popular Religion in Vietnam* (Honolulu: University of Hawai'i Press, 2004).

19. Ornit Shani, *Communalism, Caste and Hindu Nationalism: The Violence in Gujarat* (Cambridge: Cambridge University Press, 2007).

20. See also Christopher J. Fuller, *The Camphor Flame: Popular Hinduism and Society in India* (Princeton: Princeton University Press, 2004).

21. Thomas Blom Hansen, *The Saffron Wave: Democracy and Hindu Nationalism in Modern India* (Princeton: Princeton University Press, 1999).

22. For a broad overview of this shifting pattern of religious violence in Indonesia, see John T. Sidel, *Riots, Pogroms, Jihad: Religious Violence in Indonesia* (Ithaca: Cornell University Press, 2006).

23. On this trend, see, for example, "Islam Sebagai Baju Zirah di Kalangan Muda", *Tempo*, 13 May 1989.

24. Asna Hasin, "Philosophical and Sociological Aspects of Da'wah: A Study of Dewan Dakwah Islamiyah Indonesia" (Ph.D. dissertation, Columbia University, 1998).

25. On these trends, see Robert W. Hefner, "Islam, State, and Civil Society: ICMI and the Struggle for the Indonesian Middle Class", *Indonesia* 56 (October 1993): 1–35; and R. William Liddle, "The

Islamic Turn in Indonesia: A Political Explanation", *Journal of Asian Studies* 55, no. 3 (August 1996): 613–34.

26. Of the 153 members of the PDI-P elected to the DPR in 1999, only 96 (63 per cent) were registered as Muslims, with at least 36 Protestants (23 per cent), 12 Catholics, and 7 Hindus among the remaining MPs. See *Wajah Dewan Perwakilan Rakyat Republik Indonesia Pemilihan Umum 1999* (Jakarta: Kompas, 2000), pp. 3–155.

27. Nadirsyah Hosen, "Religion and the Indonesian Constitution: A Recent Debate", *Journal of Southeast Asian Studies* 36, no. 3 (October 2005).

28. Julia Day Howell, "Sufism and the Indonesian Islamic Revival", *Journal of Asian Studies* 60, no. 3 (2001). See also: "Berputar Menuju Sang Kekasih", *Tempo*, 28 May 2006.

29. See, for example, "Beribu Jalan Menyenangkan Tuhan Dan Umat", *Tempo*, 5 November 2006 and the related articles on individual *kyai* in the same issue.

30. See, for example, "Kepahitan Pengikut Sanghyang Kersa", *Tempo*, 20 August 2006 and "Setelah Cap Pembangkang Dilekatkan", *Tempo*.

31. Julia Day Howell, "Muslims, the New Age and Marginal Religions in Indonesia: Changing Meanings of Religious Pluralism", *Social Compass* 52, no. 4 (2005).

32. On the MUI and its various *fatwa* of recent years, see John R. Bowen, *Islam, Law and Equality in Indonesia: An Anthropology of Public Reasoning* (Cambridge: Cambridge University Press, 2003); and Moch. Nur Ichwan, "'Ulamā', State and Politics: Majelis Ulama Indonesia After Suharto", *Islamic Law and Society* 12, no. 1 (2005). See also "MUI to formulate edicts against 'liberal thoughts' ", *Jakarta Post*, 27 July 2005; "Fatwa MUI Memicu Kontroversi; Ma'ruf Amin: MUI Siap Menanggapi", *Kompas*, 30 July 2005.

33. For an extensive treatment of the competing sources of *fatwa* in Indonesia, see M.B. Hooker, *Indonesian: Islam: Social Change Through Contemporary Fatāwān* (Honolulu: University of Hawai'i Press, 2003).

34. "Playboy Indonesia: Modest Flesh Meets Muslim Faith", *New York Times*, 24 July 2006.

35. "Undang-Undang Dengan Definisi Kabur", *Tempo*, 12 February 2006.

36. "Goyangan Tak Kunjung Reda", *Tempo*, 14 May 2006, pp. 34–35; "Indonesian Dancer, Clerics Go Toe-to-Toe", *Asia Times*, 21 June 2006.

37. Charles Tripp, *Islam and the Moral Economy: The Challenge of Capitalism* (Cambridge: Cambridge University Press, 2006).

38. Ibid., pp. 168–69.

39. On this issue, see Suzanne Brenner, "Reconstructing Self and Society: Javanese Muslim Women and 'The Veil' ", *American Ethnologist* 23, no. 4 (November 1996). For a flavour of public discussions at the time, see also "Penerapan Jilbab Tunggu SK Dirjen", *Surabaya Post*, 18 February 1991; and "Aini, Arti, Nurul, dan Widy: Bersyukur Meski Harus Tergusur", *Surabaya Post*, 24 February 1991.

40. Suzanne Brenner, "Islam and Gender Politics in Late New Order Indonesia", in *Spirited Politics: Religion and Public Life in Contemporary Southeast Asia*, edited by Andrew C. Wilford and Kenneth M. George (Ithaca: Cornell University Southeast Asia Program, 2005); and Nancy J. Smith-Hefner, "The New Muslim Romance: Changing Patterns of Courtship and Marriage among Educated Javanese Youth", *Journal of Southeast Asian Studies* 36, no. 3 (October 2005).

41. On these trends, see, for example, Diane L. Wolf, *Factory Daughters: Gender, Household Dynamics and Rural Industrialization on Java* (Berkeley: University of California Press, 1992); and Linda Rae Bennett, *Women, Islam and Modernity: Single Women, Sexuality and Reproductive Health in Contemporary Indonesia* (London: RoutledgeCurzon, 2005).

42. On these recent trends, see, for example, Susan Blackburn, "Women and the Nation", *Inside Indonesia*, April–June 2001; and Krishna Sen, "Film Revolution? Women are now on both sides of the camera", *Inside Indonesia*, July–September 2005.

43. Pieternella van Doorn-Harder, *Women Shaping Islam: Reading the Qur'an in Indonesia* (Urbana: University of Illinois Press, 2003).

44. Julia I. Suryakusuma, "The State and Sexuality in New Order Indonesia", in *Fantasizing the Feminine in Indonesia*, edited by Laurie Sears (Durham: Duke University Press, 1996).

45. See Tom Boellstorff, "The Emergence of Political Homophobia in Indonesia: Masculinity and National Belonging", *Ethnos* 69, no. 4 (December 2004): 465–86; Tom Boellstorff, "Between Religion and Desire: Being Muslim and Gay in Indonesia", *American Anthropologist* 107, no. 4 (2005): 575–85; and Tom Boellstorff, *The Gay Archipelago: Sexuality and Nation in Indonesia* (Princeton: Princeton University Press, 2005).

46. Dédé Oetomo, "Gay Men in the Reformasi Era: Homophobic Violence could be a By-Product of the New Openness", *Inside Indonesia*, April–June 2001.

47. For early English-language assessments, see "Indonesian Islamist Party is Quietly Gaining Ground", *International Herald Tribune*, 8 April 2004; and "An Islamic Leader Rises in Indonesian Politics", *International Herald Tribune*, 21 October 2004.

48. For background, see Aay Muhamad Furkon, *Partai Keadilan Sejahtera: Ideologi dan Praksis Politik Kaum Muda Muslim Indonesia Kontemporer* (Jakarta: Teraju, 2004). Ali Said Damanik, *Fenomena Partai Keadilan: Transformasi 20 Tahun Gerakan Tarbiyah di Indonesia* (Jakarta: Teraju, 2000).

49. For recent treatments of the impact of electoral engagement on Islamist political parties and movements, see Vickie Langohr, "Of Islamists and Ballot Boxes: Rethinking the Relationship between Islamists and Electoral Politics", *International Journal of Middle East Studies* 33 (November 2001); Quintan Wiktorowicz, *The Management of Islamic Activism: Salafis, the Muslim Brotherhood, and State Power in Jordan* (Albany: SUNY Press, 2001); R. Quinn Mecham, "From the Ashes of Virtue, a Promise of Light: The Transformation of Political Islam in Turkey", *Third World Quarterly* 25, no. 2 (2004); Janine A. Clark, "The Conditions of Islamist Moderation: Unpacking Cross-Ideological Cooperation in Jordan", *International Journal of Middle East Studies* 38 (2006); and Jillian Schwedler, *Faith in Moderation: Islamist Parties in Jordan and Yemen* (Cambridge: Cambridge University Press, 2006).

50. See, for example, "Hidayat: PKS Tidak Akan Masuk Kabinet", *Tempo Interaktif*, 26 April 2004; "Usulkan 'Reshuffle' Tim Ekonomi, PKS Tetap Loyal kepada Pemerintah", *Pikiran Rakyat*, 28 November 2005; "PKS dan PAN dukung Boediono Masuk Kabinet", *Tempo Interaktif*, 2 December 2005.

51. For recent Indonesian media coverage of the PKS' public profile, see, for example, "Partai Dakwah di Simpang Jalan", *Tempo*, 7 August 2005; "Menakar Citra, Mendukung SBY", *Tempo*, 27 November 2005; and "Wawancara: Yang Tidak Suka Syariat Berlindung di Balik Pancasila", *Tempo*, 25 June 2006.

52. "Indonesian Democracy's Enemy Within", *The Nation* (Bangkok), 5 December 2005.

53. For broader arguments along these lines, see Olivier Roy, *Globalised Islam: The Search for a New Ummah* (London: Hurst & Company, 2004), pp. 72–83; Vali Nasr, "The Rise of 'Muslim Democracy' ", *Journal of Democracy* 16, no. 2 (April 2005): 13–27. See also Stathis Kalyvas, *Religious Mobilization and Party Formation: Confessional Parties and the Christian Democratic Phenomenon* (Ithaca: Cornell University Press, 1996).

54. For recent coverage, see, for example, "Aneka Ragam Laskar Jalanan", *Gatra*, 15 June 2006; and "Laskar-Laskar Dalam Sorotan", *Tempo*, 25 June 2006.

55. See "Pengurus PGI Temui Presiden SBY Minta Usut Tuntas Penutupan Paksa Gereja", *Sinar Indonesia Baru*, 25 August 2005; "Sebatang Salib yang Dikunci", *Tempo*, 5 September 2005; "Police Investigate Church Closures, Vow to Take Action", *Jakarta Post*, 13 September 2005.

56. See, for example, "Soal Lama, Ketegangan Baru", *Tempo*, 20 August 2006, pp. 62–65; "Setelah Cambukan 40 Kali", *Tempo*, 20 August 2006.

57. See, for example, "Gelora Syariah Mengepung Kota", *Gatra*, 6 May 2006, pp. 20–24; "Menguji Niat Baik Perda", *Gatra*, 6 May 2006; "Syariat Islam di Jalur Lambat", *Tempo*, 14 May 2006; "Akibat Menyontek Tetangga", *Tempo*, 14 May 2006, p. 32; "Pecut Bambu

Dari Bulukumba", *Tempo*, 14 May 2006. See also *Islamic Law and Criminal Justice in Aceh* (Jakarta/Brussels: International Crisis Group, July 2006).

58. See "Jika Malam Selalu Mencemaskan", *Tempo*, 14 May 2006; and "Women caught in a more Radical Indonesia", *New York Times*, 28 June 2006.

59. On the absence of violent conflict in multi-faith communities in various localities around the Indonesian archipelago, see, for example, "Ketika Batas Religi Meleleh", *Tempo*, 20 August 2006; "Azan Magrib di Bali", *Tempo*, 20 August 2006; "Hidup Rukun di Lembah Dumoga", *Tempo*, 20 August 2006.

60. J. Vernon Henderson and Ari Kuncoro, "Sick of Local Government Corruption? Vote Islamic", *NBER Working Paper 12110* (Cambridge, MA: National Bureau of Economic Research, March 2006).

61. Elizabeth Fuller Collins, "Islam and the Habits of Democracy: Islamic Organizations in Post-New Order South Sumatra", *Indonesia* 78 (October 2004).

62. Hamdan Juhannis, "The Struggle for Formalist Islam in South Sulawesi: From Darul Islam (DI) to Komite Persiapan Penegakan Syariat Islam" (Ph.D. dissertation, Australian National University, 2006).

63. Julian Barnes, *Nothing to be Frightened of* (London: Jonathan Cape, 2008).

64. Charles Taylor, *A Secular Age* (Cambridge: Harvard University Press, 2007).

INDEX

A

Aa Gym, 160

Abdurrahman Wahid, 171, 173–74

Abraham, J., 101

Accenture, 4

Adams, M. D., 91

adat, 173

Africa, 139, 147

Aghion, Philippe, 126

agriculture, 125

Ahmadiyya mosques, 168

air pollution, 127

Al-Qur'an, 163

All-Indonesian Association of
Islamic Intellectuals (ICMI),
170

Amazon, 120

American College of Medical
Genetics, 94

American Economic Association,
150n1

American Economic Review, 150n1

Amgen, 94

Amien Rais, 171, 177

Anderson, Dennis, 151n11

Anderson, J. F., 132

Angell, M., 97–98

Anger, Niels, 145

Angkor, 13

Ariad Pharmaceuticals, 93–94

Aristotle, 37

Arrhenius, Svante, 150n2

Asia. *See also* Emerging Asia
ancient civilisations, 2, 13
biotech sector, 80, 84
challenges to knowledge
economies, 7–10, 14
expansion of education, 156
human rights and free speech,
31, 46
illicit trade in organs, 87
patriarchal societies, 51, 157
political power in, 157–58
poverty alleviation, 15
relations with West, 12–13,
31–32
religion and society, 23–26,
156–66, 183–85

shift of global power to, 12–
    13, 15, 58–59, 61, 64
urbanization, 23, 160, 163,
    169
Asian Financial Crisis (AFC), 15,
    31, 57, 61
Asian values, 21–22, 35, 42–52
Association of University
    Technology Managers, 86
Augustine, Saint, 38
Australia, 137, 139, 148
automotive industry, 132
Axis powers, 40

B
Bahasa Indonesia, 163
Bali, 136–38, 148, 166, 168
Baltimore, David, 94
Bandung, 178
Bangkok, 161
Bangkok Declaration, 21, 44–47
Bangladesh, 77n1
Barnes, Julian, 184
Bayh-Dole Amendments, 85–86
Beijing, 22, 53, 157
Beijing University, 3
Bengali language, 163
Bentham, Jeremy, 37
biodiversity, 123–24, 127
bioeconomy, 79, 83–84, 101
biomedical research, 6, 16–17,
    83, 85, 87
biomedicine, 83–84, 88, 92,
    101–02

BIONET, 81
Biopolis, 80, 103n3
biotechnology industry, 17, 19,
    79, 84, 87, 90
BJP (Bharatiya Janata Party), 167
Blair, Tony, 91
Body of Christ, 161
Bonn, 144
border taxes, 132
Boyle, James, 85, 92, 101–02
Brown, Gordon, 137
Buddhism, 159–61, 166, 184
Burke, Edmund, 37
Burma, 157, 185
business process outsourcing
    (BPO), 3–4

C
California, 137
Cambodia, 13, 77n1, 157
Canada, 73, 74f, 75, 84, 94, 139
Cao Dai, 160
capital, 67, 69–71
capitalism, 40
carbon cycle, 112, 118, 120, 125
carbon dioxide, 112
carbon dioxide equivalents
    (CO_2e), 117
carbon emissions. *See* greenhouse
    gas (GHG) emissions
carbon neutrality, 137
carbon pricing
    marginal abatement cost
        (MAC), 116, 124–27

marginal GHG damages, 116
mechanisms, 129–33
policy focus, 29, 115, 128
reduction targets and, 117
carbon sinks, 120
carbon taxation, 129–30, 132–33
carbon trading, 129–32, 136,
    142–46, 148
Cassels, A., 97
Catholic Church, 37–38, 159–62
Caulfield, T., 95
CCS (carbon capture and
    storage), 132, 138, 143t,
    144, 146
Cebu, 160
Celera Genomics, 90–91
cell lines, 88
Central Electricity Generation
    Board (UK), 151n7
Central Sulawesi, 168, 181
Chakrabarty, Ananda, 89
Chen Shaohua, 77
China
    ancient achievements, 2, 13
    biomedical sector, 81
    Communist Party, 53, 157
    contribution to global
        economy, 15, 62
    economic growth, 1, 3, 12, 61,
        69, 71
    education, 2–3, 16, 64
    gene patenting and, 93
    greenhouse gas emissions, 31,
        119, 139

high-tech sector, 4
human rights, 22
in Emerging Asia, 77n1
internal security, 9
manufacturing sector, 4
political protests against, 9,
    22–23, 53
poverty alleviation, 15, 65–66,
    76
public perceptions in, 148
religion in, 24, 158–60, 166,
    184
science and technology, 2
Chinese diaspora, 160
Chinese language, 4–5, 9
Cho, M. K., 95
Christian Democrats, 180
Christianity, 160–61, 166, 168,
    184
Cicero, 37
Clean Development Mechanism
    (CDM), 144
climate change. See also
    greenhouse gas (GHG)
    emissions; greenhouse gases
    (GHG)
    adaptation, 147
    consequences, 26, 28, 111–13,
        120–21
    economic policy and, 27–28
    global nature, 29, 135
    modelling, 118–22, 150n3
    projections, 30–31
    rates, 113

scientific evidence, 113, 123–
        24
shared knowledge and, 26, 29,
        135
time lags, 113
under business-as-usual, 113,
        150n4
climate change economics. *See
        also* carbon pricing
cost-benefit analyses, 111,
        117, 123, 127, 132–34,
        145
importance, 148
knowledge and, 115, 122, 133
modelling, 116–17
price and quantity tools, 115,
        129
risk analysis, 111, 113–24,
        149–50
climate change policy
criteria, 135–36, 138, 147, 149
equity issues, 111, 114, 116,
        125, 130–31, 136–47,
        151n9
financing, 142–43, 145
incentive structure, 127, 134
international, 29–31, 114, 128,
        130–32, 135–37, 141–47
public and, 115, 128, 134,
        136, 148
ramp, 122, 127
regulations and standards,
        129, 132
resistance from industry, 132

stock targets *vs.* pricing, 115
technology and, 28, 128–29,
        133–36, 143–44, 146
tradable quotas, 130–31
urgency, 127–28, 149–50
climate history, 120–21
climate sensitivity, 112–13, 118
Clinton, Bill, 91
coal, 129, 132, 143t, 146
Cold War, 180
Communist Asia, 24, 53, 158
Computable General Equilibrium
        Models (CGMs), 116
conflicts, 121
Congress Party (India), 167
Copernicus, 2
Costa Rica, 137
Council of Indonesian Islamic
        Scholars, 173–74
Crisologo, Vincent "Bingbong",
        161

D
Darwin, Charles, 35
Davao, 160
Davies, S. M., 96
Davis, P. K., 92
Declaration of the Rights of Man
        and of the Citizen, 37, 39
Dédé Oetomo, 177
deforestation
combatting, 126–27
policy on, 128, 136, 143t, 148
share of emissions, 125, 145

Delanty, Gerard, 32n1
Demaine, L. T., 88
democracy, 52–54, 128
Democratic Party (Partai
    Demokrat), 177
Denmark, 81–82
Department of Environment,
    Food and Rural Affairs
    (DEFRA), 151n10
Diamond *vs.* Chakrabarty, 89
diniyah, 169
DNA sequencing, 88, 90–92, 95
drug licensing, 98
drug patents, 94, 97
drug trials, 98–101

E
East Asian Tiger economies, 58,
    61, 69, 72. *See also* Asia;
    Emerging Asia
economic growth, 67–72, 76–77
Edinburgh patent, 90
education, 2–3, 72–76, 156, 169
Egypt, 178, 180
El Shaddai, 160–62
electricity generation, 125–26,
    130, 133, 146
Eli Lilly & Company, 94
Elliot, C., 97
Emerging Asia
    Asian financial crisis and, 61
    definition, 77n1
    economic importance, 15–16,
        58, 60–61

educational achievement, 72–76
    LSE student body and, 63–64
    poverty alleviation, 15, 64–66
    sources of growth, 67–72
Enbrel, 94
energy access, 127
energy efficiency, 28, 125–26,
    128
energy security, 127
England, 37, 121
English language, 4–6, 9
Enkvist, Per-Anders, 145
Enlightenment, 2, 35, 38, 42
Eocene, 121
EPA (Environmental Protection
    Agency), 132
Epictetus, 37
Ernst & Young, 84
Estonia, 75
Euro-Communists, 180
Europe
    biotech sector, 84, 93
    carbon emissions, 139
    history of science, 82–83
    illicit trade in organs, 87
    knowledge-based bioeconomy,
        81
    patent system, 89
    religion and politics, 180
European Convention on
    Human Rights and
    Fundamental Freedoms, 40
European Patent Office (EPO),
    89–90, 95

European Spring Council, 138
European Union Emissions
    Trading Scheme (EUETS),
    130–31, 144
expressed sequence tags (ESTs), 90

F
Falun Gong, 160
Fankhauser, Samuel, 127
fatwa, 163, 173–74
Fellmeth, A. X., 88
Finland, 73–76
Fitna, 8, 26
Foucault, Michel, 13–14, 19–20
Fourier, Joseph, 150n2
Fourth Assessment Report of
    IPCC, 113, 119
FPI (Front Pembela Islam), 25,
    168, 180, 182
France, 37, 73–75f, 95, 137
    free speech
    democracy and, 52–54
    human rights and, 16, 21, 39,
        41–42
    in Asia, 31
    knowledge and, 19, 34
    limits on, 22, 54
    political autonomy and, 35
    religion and, 35
Friedman, Thomas L., 69
Front for the Defenders of Islam,
    25, 168, 180, 182
Front Pembela Islam (FPI), 25,
    168, 180, 182
Fujian province, 158

G
G7 economies, 15–16, 60, 63,
    67–70, 77n1
G8 Gleneagles summit, 30, 143t,
    147
G8-G5 summit, 136
Galileo, 2
Garnaut Review, 137–38
Gaza Strip, 180
Gearty, Conor, 16, 19–22
gender, 43, 174–75
gene patenting
    concerns, 18, 88, 92–97
    creating monopolies, 86
    debate in USA, 90
    disease and, 93–95
    guidelines, 91
general circulation models
    (GCMs), 118–19
genetic engineering, 90
genomics, 88, 93, 95–96
Germany, 54, 73–75f, 136, 138
Gleneagles summit, 30, 143t, 147
global climate models (GCMs),
    118–19
global economy
    biomedical sector, 84, 93
    climate change and, 117, 125–
        26
    contribution of Emerging Asia,
        60–61
    growth, 125–26
    underperformance, 59–60
Global North, 36–38, 40, 42, 45,
    51, 53

global warming, 112–13, 118–19.
    See also climate change
globalization, 9–10
Goh Keng Swee, 1
Gold, E. R., 88
Goldstein, D. B., 96
GOLKAR, 25, 181–83
Google, 4
Gottweis, H., 81
greenhouse effect, 113
greenhouse gas (GHG) emissions
    across sectors, 125, 144
    as externalities, 111, 114, 127,
        129, 133
    country by country, 31, 119, 139
    flow targets, 116
    global per capita, 138
    Heiligendamm targets for, 30,
        136–37, 142t
    history of flows, 138, 141, 147
    link to warming, 112, 114, 118
    measurement, 129
    reduction targets, 115, 131,
        137–38
    sources, 112
    stabilization targets, 114–17,
        123–25, 138
    under business-as-usual, 120,
        124–25, 139, 144, 146
greenhouse gas (GHG) stocks
    as externalities, 27
    positive feedbacks, 120
    role in climate change, 112,
        114–15, 118
    stabilizing, 123–24, 140

greenhouse gases (GHG), 112–
    13, 119–20, 137

H
Habibie, B. J., 170–71, 180
Hadley Centre, 119, 122
halaqah, 169
Hanoi, 157
Harvard University, 89, 93
Hassan Al-Banna, 178
Healy, D., 97
Heath, D., 93
Heiligendamm emissions targets,
    30, 136–37, 142t
Henry, C., 115
HFCs (hydrofluorocarbons), 112
Hidayat Nur Wahid, 177–78
Himalayas, 121
Hinduism, 160–61, 164, 166–67,
    184
Hindutva, 167
Hirschhorn, J. N., 96
Hoa Hao, 160
Hobbes, Thomas, 37
Holland, 8, 26
Holmes, Oliver Wendell, 35
homosexuality, 176–77
Hong Kong, 61, 69, 73–76, 77n1
Hsieh Chang-tai, 77n2
Hu Jintao, 157
Huawei, 4
Human Genome Project, 88, 90–
    92
human life, 121
human resources, 7–8

human rights
  abuse of concept, 36, 50
  American power and, 21, 40
  Asian values and, 21–22, 35,
    42–52
  China and, 22, 53
  free speech and, 16, 20
  fundamental principles, 41–42,
    48–50
  gender and, 43–44, 51
  intellectual property and, 102
  international law, 39, 41, 46
  philosophy of, 37–38
  reformulation, 40
  universality of, 20–22, 34–37,
    40–42, 52–55
  Western origins, 36–40, 47
  Western statehood and, 38
Hwang Woo-Suk, 81, 84

I
IAIN (Institut Agama Islam
    Negeri), 169, 177
ICMI (All-Indonesian Association
    of Islamic Intellectuals), 170
IEA (International Energy
    Agency), 126
Iloilo, 160
India
  ancient achievements, 2, 13
  business process outsourcing
    (BPO), 3–4
  contribution to global
    economy, 15, 62
  corruption, 157

economic growth, 1, 3, 12, 61,
    69, 71
education, 2–3, 16, 64
gene patenting and, 93
greenhouse gas emissions, 31,
    139
high-tech sector, 4
Hinduism in, 161, 164, 167
in Emerging Asia, 77n1
poverty alleviation, 65–66
public perceptions in, 148
religious violence, 166–67
science and technology, 2
Indian Institute of Technology
    (IIT), 3
Indonesia
  Constitution, 171, 179
  corruption, 157
  economy, 61
  globalized terrorism in, 168
  greenhouse gas emissions, 31
  homosexuality in, 176–77
  in Emerging Asia, 77n1
  Islam in, 161, 163, 166–83
  local politics, 180–82
  New Order Government, 172
  non-Muslims in, 168, 171,
    179, 181
  religion and politics in, 23–26,
    160, 167–83
  violence, 166, 168, 181, 183
  women in, 174–76, 179, 181
Indonesian Democratic Party of
    Struggle (PDI-P), 25, 171,
    181–83

Industrial Revolution, 2, 13
Information Age, 157
information and
    communications technology
    (ICT), 16, 23, 26, 31, 67–70,
    72
information economy. *See*
    knowledge economies
Infosys, 4
Institut Agama Islam Negeri
    (IAIN), 169, 177
Institut Curie, 95
Institute of Technical Education
    (Singapore), 5
intellectual property rights
    effects on knowledge, 18, 87,
        104n7
    gene patenting and, 93
    private capital and, 85
    public good and, 101–02,
        104n7
    respect for, 7
International Covenant on Civil
    and Political Rights, 39
International Covenant on
    Economic, Social and
    Cultural Rights, 39
Internet, 6, 8–9, 92, 126, 156
IPCC (International Panel on
    Climate Change), 113, 119
Islam
    ancient civilisation, 13
    education, 169
    gender and, 174–77, 181
    in Indonesia, 24–25, 167–83

    in southern Thailand, 167
    Internet and, 163
    militant, 162
    mysticism in, 163–64, 172
    new definitions, 160, 162,
        166, 170, 173–75
    terrorism and, 166, 183
Islamabad, 166
IT (information technology), 7
Italy, 73–75f

J
Jakarta, 160, 168, 172, 175, 177–
    78, 181
Japan, 15, 60, 67, 73, 74f, 75,
    139, 157
Jaringan Islam Liberal (JIL), 174
Java, 13
jihad, 168
JIL (Jaringan Islam Liberal), 174
Jordan, B., 95
Jorgensen, Dale, 69, 77n2

K
Kant, Immanuel, 38, 41
Kass, Leon, 87
Kay, L. E., 84
Kelley, J. J., 92
Kendall, T., 98
Kennedy, D., 85
knowledge. *See also* scientific
        knowledge
    ancient civilisations, 2, 13
    authority and, 34, 158, 164
    commercialisation, 16, 19, 81

control, 23–26, 174, 183–84
economic driver, as, 14–16
education and, 72–76
human rights and, 16
Orientalist approach, 14
power and, 14, 20, 38, 156–58,
    169, 173, 185
protection, 16–19, 83, 87,
    105n7
religion and, 23–26, 158, 160–
    61, 163, 165–66
sharing, 26–31, 82, 86, 135
social construction, 13–14, 19,
    35, 40, 84, 102, 184
technology and, 67, 72, 133
trust and, 82, 100, 102–03,
    136
uncertainty and, 115
knowledge economies
challenges, 7–10
conditions for growing, 3, 6–7,
    10, 12
definition, 32n1
economic growth and, 1
human resources and, 7–8
in Asia, 1–5, 7–10, 14
in Singapore, 5–7
knowledge society. *See*
    knowledge economies
Krugman, Paul, 58
kyai, 25, 172
Kyoto Protocol, 119, 137, 144

L
labour, 7–8, 67–70
Lakoff, A., 101
land use, 125
Lander, E. S., 91
Laos, 157
Laskar Jihad, 168
Latour, B., 83
LDP (Liberal Democratic Party,
    Japan), 157
Lee Hsien Loong, 12–13, 15, 17,
    22, 26, 31
Lee Kuan Yew, 44
Lenovo, 4
Liberal Islam Network, 174
life expectancy, 127
Linton, L. M., 91
literacy, 163
Locke, John, 37, 50
Lockeian principle of property
    rights, 88
London, U.K., 3, 121
Loved Flock, The, 161
low-carbon technology, 134
LSE (London School of
    Economics), 1, 62–64, 81
LSE Asia Forum 2008, 1, 12, 14,
    156

M
Macau-China, 73
MacLeod, C., 83
madrasas, 164

Magna Carta, 37
Mahathir bin Mohamad, 44
Mahbubani, Kishore, 12, 32
Majelis Permusyawaratan Rakyat (MPR), 177
Majelis Ulama Indonesia (MUI), 173–74
Makassar, 160
Malay language, 4, 163
Malaysia, 4, 44, 77n1, 157, 166
Maluku, 168, 181
Manila, 160, 162
Manolio, T. A., 96
marginal abatement costs (MAC), 116, 124–27
Marx, Karl, 37
McCain, John, 138
McGoey, L., 98–99
McGuire, A. L., 95
McKinsey cost curve, 145, 151n11
medicine, 85
Medicines and Healthcare Regulatory Authority (MHRA), 98, 100
Megawati Soekarnoputri, 171
Meinshausen, M., 119
Mendelsohn, Robert, 122
methane, 112, 120
Mexico, 93
Middle East, 178
Mill, John Stuart, 128
Millennium Development Goals, 147

Ministry for the Empowerment of Women, 176
MIT (Massachusetts Institute of Technology), 3, 93
Monte Carlo estimates, 119, 122
Monterrey commitment, 30, 143t, 147
Moore, John, 88
Morocco, 178
motor industry, 132
Moynihan, R., 97
MPR (Majelis Permusyawaratan Rakyat), 177
Muhammadiyah, 161–62, 169, 171, 176–77
MUI (Majelis Ulama Indonesia), 173–74
Murrow, Edward R., 82–83
Muslim Brotherhood, 178
Muslims, 8, 26, 160–61, 170–71, 175, 184
Myers, Erin C., 145
Myriad Genetics, 94

N
Nahdlatul Ulama, 161–62, 169, 171, 173, 176
National Awakening Party (PKB), 171
National Coal Board (UK), 151n7
National Institute of Health, 100
National Mandate Party (PAN), 171, 177

Nature (journal), 91, 94
Needham, Joseph, 2
Needham, Roger, 86
Nepal, 77n1
Nepstad, Daniel, 145
Netherlands, 76
New Orleans, 150n1
New York, 121
New York Times, 94
New Zealand, 73, 75, 137
Newton, Isaac, 2
nitrous oxide, 112
non-governmental organizations
    (NGO), 47
Nordhaus, William D., 122
North Korea, 157
North Maluku, 168, 181
Norway, 137
Novartis, 100
Novas, C., 81, 97
nuclear power, 133

O
Obama, Barack, 138
oceans, 120
OECD (Organization for
    Economic Cooperation and
    Development), 72–76, 147
Olympic torch protest, 8–9, 22,
    53
OncoMouse, 89
Ong Dia, 159
Ong, A., 79
organ trades, 85, 87

Orosa, Ramon, 161
overseas Chinese, 160
Overseas Development
    Assistance (ODA), 30, 143t,
    145, 147

P
Pakistan, 77n1, 157, 163, 178, 180
PAN (National Mandate Party),
    171, 177
Pancasila, 171
Partai Amanat Nasional, 171
Partai Demokrasi Indonesia —
    Perjuangan (PDI-P), 25, 171,
    181–83
Partai Demokrat, 177
Partai Keadilan Sejahtera (PKS),
    177–78, 179–80, 182
patents. *See also* gene patenting;
    intellectual property rights
    anti-commons nature, 17–18,
       93–94, 105n7
    as compensation, 17, 83, 98,
       135
    on drugs, 97
    on life, 88–92, 105n13
    on tests, 94–95
    requirements, 91
    rush to translation, 96–97
    scientific research and, 85–87
Paul, Saint, 37–38
PDI-P (Partai Demokrasi
    Indonesia — Perjuangan),
    25, 171, 181–83

Pearson, T. A., 96
pengajian, 164, 169
People's Action Party (PAP), 157
People's Consultative Assembly, 177
petroleum products, 129
Petryna, A., 101
pharmaceutical corporations, 18–19, 93–94, 96–101
pharmacogenomics, 96
Philippines, 77n1, 157, 161–62, 167
Phnom Penh, 157
photovoltaics, 134
PISA (Programme for International Student Assessment), 72–76, 77n3
PKB (National Awakening Party), 171
PKS (Partai Keadilan Sejahtera), 25, 177–80, 182
Plato, 37
Playboy magazine, 174
Plotinus, 37
population, 138–39
Poso, 181
post-modernism, 13–14, 35, 41–42
poverty alleviation, 64–66, 69, 76, 102
power generation, 125–26, 130, 133, 146
property rights, 88
Prosperous Justice Party, 25, 177–80, 182

Protestantism, 160, 162, 168, 171
public health, 98–99, 101–02
public-private collaboration, 134
Pyongyang, 157

Q
qigong, 160
Quah, Danny, 15–16
Quan Am, 159
Qur'an, 163

R
Rangoon, 185
Rapp, R., 93
Ravallion, Martin, 77
Ready, T., 94
recombinant DNA technology, 89
religion
    democratization of, 23, 25–26, 158–66, 168, 184–85
    gender and, 174–76, 181
    mass media and, 160–64, 173
    popular, 165
    violence and, 166–68, 181
Relman, A. S., 98
renewable energy, 132, 138
research and development, 6, 17, 79, 134, 151n7
Rheinberger, H.-J., 84
Richard Ely Lecture, 150n1
Rose, Nikolas, 16–19, 81, 84
Rousseau, Jean-Jacques, 37, 50

Roy, Olivier, 163
Royal Society of London, 86
Rudd, Kevin, 137

S
Said, Edward, 14, 32
Salafism, 160–61
Salk, Jonas, 82
sangha, 161–62
Sathaye, Jayant, 145
Scheper-Hughes, N., 85
Science (journal), 91
scientific commons, 83, 85
scientific knowledge
  as property, 83, 86
  compromised, 86, 93
  education, 2–3, 72–76
  nature of, 82–84
  public domain and, 83, 91–92,
    102
Scott, R., 88
Second World War, 38–40
Shaanxi province, 158
Shanmugaratnam, Tharman, 1
Shapin, Steven, 82, 102
shari'a law, 162, 181–82
Sharp, Phillip A., 94
Sherwood, T., 132
Sidel, John, 23–26
Silicon Valley, 3
Singapore
  "brain drain" and, 10
  Asian financial crisis, 58
  Asian identity, 7

Asian values debate, 44
biotech sector, 17, 79–80
citizens abroad, 1, 10
East Asian Tiger, 61
economic growth, 69–70, 72
Economic Review Committee,
  58
education in, 5, 8, 77n3
English language in, 6
global links *vs.* national
  priorities, 6, 10–11
in Emerging Asia, 77n1
knowledge economy, 5–7, 11
PAP government, 157
research and development in,
  6, 17, 79
societal ethos, 6–7
Smith, Adam, 35
Smith, J.S., 82
socialism, 40
Soeharto, 168–70, 172, 176
South Korea, 61, 69, 73–76,
  77n1, 84
South Sulawesi, 181–82
Southeast Asia, 4–5, 13
Sri Lanka, 77n1
Srivijaya, 13
Stainforth, D., 122
State Islamic Institute (IAIN),
  169, 177
Stehr, Nico, 32
stem cells, 90
Stern Review, 26, 117–19, 124–
  25, 147

Stern, Nicholas, 26–31, 115,
    118–19, 125, 128, 137
Sufism, 160–61, 163, 172
Sulawesi, 168, 181
Sulston, John, 90
Surabaya, 160
Susilo Bambang Yudhoyono,
    171, 177–78

T
Taiwan, 61, 69, 72, 74–76, 77n1,
    157, 159
Tangerang, 181
tarekat, 163–64
Tata, 4
Tate, S. K., 96
Taussig, K. S., 93
taxation, 129–30, 133
Taylor, Charles, 185
technology
  climate change and, 115, 128,
      133, 135, 143–44
  economic growth and, 67, 72,
      77
  patents and, 89–90
  religion and, 160, 173
  terrorism, 8, 35
Tet, 159
Thailand, 57, 61, 73–75f, 77n1,
    157, 161, 167
Than Tai, 159
Theravada Buddhism, 161
Thomas Aquinas, Saint, 37–38
Tibetans, 9, 23, 53

total factor productivity (TFP),
    67–72
trade policy, 116–17, 131
transgenic organisms, 89
translational medicine, 17, 80
transport, 125–26
Triendl, R., 81
Triggle, D. J., 94, 98
Tripp, Charles, 175
Tsinghua University, 157
Turkey, 178, 180
Tyndall, John, 150n2

U
UMNO (United Malays National
    Organization), 157
UN Financing for Development,
    147
UNDP (United Nations
    Development Program), 147
UNESCO, 88, 105n8
UNFCCC (United Nations
    Framework Convention on
    Climate Change), 136
United Kingdom
  biomedical research, 90
  drug licensing, 98–99
  educational achievement, 73–75f
  emissions targets, 137
  privatization, 151n7
  universities in, 3, 63
United Nations, 40, 47, 105n8
United States of America
  biotech sector, 84, 86, 93–94

contribution to global
    economy, 15, 62
credit crisis, 57
Declaration of Independence,
    37
drug licensing, 98
educational achievement, 73–
    75f
global warming and, 138–39, 148
human rights and, 37, 54
intellectual property rights, 85
patent law, 88–89, 91–92
trade in body parts, 87–88
universities in, 3
Universal Declaration of Human
    Rights, 39–40
universities, 3, 63, 82–83, 85,
    99–100, 102
University of California Berkeley,
    100
urbanization, 23, 160, 163, 169
Urdu, 163
U.S. Board of Patent Appeals and
    Interferences, 89
U.S. Food and Drug
    Administration (FDA), 98,
    100
U.S. Patent Office, 91
U.S. Supreme Court, 89

V
VAT (value-added tax), 132

Velarde, "Brother Mike", 162
Venter, Craig, 90–91
Vienna Declaration, 43–44
Vientiane, 157
Vietnam, 4, 24, 77n1, 157–60,
    165–66, 184
Vu, Khuong, 69, 77n2

W
Wahid, Abdurrahman, 171, 173–
    74
Wahlberg, A., 98
Waquant, L., 85
Weber, Max, 82
Wellcome Trust, 90–91
West Bank, 180
West Java, 180
West, the, 13, 20–21, 36–40. *See
    also* Europe; Global North
Western Europe, 180
Whitehead Institute, 93
Whittington, C.J., 99
wind energy, 132
Wipro, 4
World Conference on Human
    Rights, 21, 43
worldliness concept, 32
WTO (World Trade
    Organization), 136

Y
Young, Alwyn, 58, 77n2

www.ingramcontent.com/pod-product-compliance
Lightning Source LLC
Chambersburg PA
CBHW021535260326
41914CB00001B/28